Small Water Enterprises in Africa
2: Kenya

Small Water Enterprises in Africa 2: Kenya

A study of small water enterprises in Nairobi

Isaack Oenga and David Kuria

Series Editors: Cyrus Njiru and Mike Smith

Water, Engineering and Development Centre
Loughborough University
2006

Water, Engineering and Development Centre,
Loughborough University,
Leicestershire, LE11 3TU, UK

© WEDC, Loughborough University, 2006

ISBN 13 Paperback: 978 1 84380 095 8
ISBN Ebook: 9781788533522
Book DOI: http://dx.doi.org/10.3362/9781788533522

A catalogue record for this book is available from the British Library.

A reference copy of this publication is also available online at:
http://www.lboro.ac.uk/wedc/publications/

Oenga, I. and Kuria, D. (2006)
Small Water Enterprises in Africa 2: Kenya
A study of small water enterprises in Nairobi

WEDC (The Water, Engineering and Development Centre) at Loughborough University in the UK is one of the world's leading institutions concerned with education, training, research and consultancy for the planning, provision and management of physical infrastructure for development in low- and middleincome countries.

This edition is reprinted and distributed by Practical Action Publishing.
Since 1974, Practical Action Publishing has published and disseminated books and information in support of international development work throughout the world. Practical Action Publishing trades only in support of its parent charity objectives and any profits are covenanted back to Practical Action (Charity Reg. No. 247257, Group VAT Registration No. 880 9924 76).

This document is an output from a project funded by the UK
Department for International Development (DFID)
for the benefit of low-income countries.
The views expressed are not necessarily those of DFID.

Designed at WEDC by Kay Davey and Glenda McMahon
Front cover photo montage by Rod Shaw
Front cover photographs by Cyrus Njiru
Illustrations by Ken Chatterton

Acknowledgements

The editors wish to express gratitude to the in-country study team comprising Izaack Oenga and David Kuria, both of ITDG Eastern Africa.

The editors wish to thank members of the UK research team comprising Mike Albu, Diana Mitlin and Gordon McGranahan, for their important role in the research project; and also to Mike Albu for his editorial contributions.

Contents

List of boxes

List of figures

List of tables

Acronyms

ASAL	Arid and semi-arid lands
CAAC	Catchment Area Advisory Committee
CBO	Community-based organization
DFID	Department for International Development
GoK	Government of Kenya
IDRC	International Development and Research Corporation
ITDG–EA	Practical Action – East Africa (formerly the Intermediate Technology Development Group (ITDG) – East Africa)
KSh	Kenyan Shilling
MDG	Millenium Development Goal
MWI	Ministry of Water and Irrigation
MWRMD	Ministry of Water Resources Management and Development
NGO	Non-government organization
NWCPC	National Water Conservation and Pipeline Corporation
NWSC	Nairobi City Water and Sewerage Company Limited
O&M	Operation and maintenance
PPP	Public–private partnership
PRSP	Poverty Reduction Strategy Paper
PSP	Private sector participation
RWS	Rural water supply
SHG	Self-help groups
SME	Small and micro-enterprises
SPSS	Statistical package for social sciences
SWE	Small water enterprise
UES	Urban environmental services
UFW	Unaccounted-for water
UNDP	United Nations Development Programme
UWS	Urban water supply
VWSA	Village Water Sellers Association
WAB	Water Appeal Board
WEDC	Water, Engineering and Development Centre, Loughborough University
WRMA	Water Resources Management Authority
WRUA	Water Resource User Association
WSB	Water Services Boards
WSD	Water and Sewerage Department
WSP	Water Service Providers
WSRB	Water Services Regulatory Board
WSRS	Water Sector Reform Secretariat
WSTF	Water Services Trust Fund

Executive Summary

Background

Phase 1 of the 'Better Access to Water in Informal Urban Settlements through Support to Small Water-Providing Enterprises' project was set up to both develop a contextual understanding and analyse the operating environment of Small Water Enterprises (SWEs); to identify, assess and select interventions to improve the performance of SWEs for Phase 2; and to begin to build a more favourable environment for SWEs through contacts with the utilities and other relevant agencies.

The research is funded by the UK Department for International Development (DFID) and is being carried out by the Water, Engineering and Development Centre (WEDC) at Loughborough University, UK. The local partner for this research is Practical Action – East Africa (formerly the Intermediate Technology Development Group (ITDG) – East Africa).

The research was conducted in Maili Saba, a typical informal settlement situated in north-eastern Nairobi with a population of nearly 10,000 people and a population density of 2,531 people per square kilometre. The overall research process adopted a case study approach due to the complexity of the issues, the significance of the context, and the lack of existing work in this area.

National context

The water sector in Kenya is characterized by continuous evolution. At independence in 1963, with a population of 6 million, the Government of Kenya embarked on an ambitious plan of providing adequate and safe water to all its people. To achieve this goal people were encouraged, in the spirit of Harambee (self-help), to invest resources to develop community-based decentralized water supply systems. In the mid-1970s the government took most of the community-managed systems back into central government administration – a move that put a large burden on public funds. The current plan is to reverse that policy by promoting decentralized,

1

participatory management systems that put the management of water systems in the hands of the users and other stakeholders.

Kenya is classified as a water-scarce country. Access to 'improved water supplies' (from house connections, public standpipes, boreholes with handpumps, protected dug wells, protected springs and rainwater collection) is estimated at over 80 per cent in urban areas and below 50 per cent in rural areas. Access to adequate water supplies for informal settlement residents is very poor and relies largely on the services of small water enterprises (SWEs).

The current water sector reforms envisage separating the function of 'Water Resources Management' and 'Water Supplies Development' and bringing in a decentralized (basin-based) management structure. The reforms confine the role of government to policy and regulation and allow for other actors to be involved in the development and management of water services. The participation of the private sector is envisaged, but may be limited to the large formal private sector, and the space for small (informal) water enterprises is not explicitly stated.

Nairobi water situation

The institutions outlined in the Water Act 2002 have been created and have started operations. The Nairobi Water Service Board is operating and has licensed the Nairobi City Water and Sewerage Company Limited (NWSC) to be the water and sewerage provider for the city of Nairobi. The company is 100 per cent owned by Nairobi City Council, and was created from the council's former water and sewerage department. Currently Nairobi's daily water production of 364,000 m³ is fully used. There is no surplus. However an estimated 50 per cent of this water is unaccounted for as a result of illegal connections and leakages from pipes. This causes serious water shortages and huge revenue losses.

Water is distributed mainly to the formal and planned settlements. The informal unplanned settlements, which are home to over 60 per cent of the city's population, do not receive any formal water services or connections. This huge population receives water from the informal small water enterprises (SWEs), who have collected their water from the utility's systems. As a result, 93 per cent of the water used in Nairobi is obtained from the utility's systems.

As part of the water sector reforms, the management of the city's water and sewerage services is now the responsibility of the newly created Nairobi City Water and Sewerage Company Limited. The company has taken bold steps to recognize and regularize the illegal water connections to the informal settlements with the twin objectives of reducing water losses and increasing revenue. These steps, however, still leave out millions of poor slum residents who are exploited by the 'better off' – those who can afford to obtain a connection and pipe into the informal settlements. The company's latest intervention is to provide a control meter chamber close to the informal settlement. SWEs (kiosk owners) will become recognized entities, and will be less prone to harassment from the utility. It remains the kiosk's responsibility to lay the piping and pump the water from the meter chamber to the point of sale (over distances of up to 1,000 m). Illegal connections used to be made with poor quality low-grade pipes. Now, however, leakages that occur between the meter and the tap are paid for by the kiosk owner, which gives them an incentive to use high-quality materials. One danger is that these higher costs might be passed on to their customers.

The informal settlements – Maili Saba

The research findings based on the literature review, field surveys (very informal interviews, focus group discussions, observations, household interviews, and triangulation workshops) and the data analysis have yielded the following conclusions.

The informal settlements offer a huge potential market for the utilities. With an average monthly income of US$70 per household, water expenditure averages US$7 a month for a household of five people. The per person water expenditure is about US$1.40 per month. With an estimated population of 1.8 million the size of the market is approximately US$2,500,000 per month at current SWE rates.

The most important water supplier in the chain in Maili Saba is the utility, which provides over 97 per cent of the water consumed here. The utility water that is sold through the kiosks accounts for 89 per cent of the total volume of water sold, as only 11 per cent is sold directly by the utility to households. These households also act as a source to their neighbours. Although most households collect their own water from the kiosk, 16 per cent buy from the tertiary SWEs – bicycles and back loaders – who buy their water from the kiosks and sell it on to households.

The mark-up in price in this chain during normal supply goes from US$0.15/m³ at the utility meter (paid by the kiosk owner) to US$2/m³ at the kiosk (paid by households who collect their water directly and by tertiary SWEs), and US$10/m³ at the domestic user level (paid by households who buy from tertiary SWEs). The figure rises to US$15/m³ for water delivered to construction sites or commercial consumers. The figures double when supply is short. The rate increases show that the labour costs of delivering water to domestic and construction consumers is indeed high, and yet a large number of consumers – 16 per cent – do buy through this route in the supply chain. This category of consumer is likely to suffer from the higher rates should the cost of water increase at the kiosks.

Key findings

SWEs

All the water to the Maili Saba slum is sold through kiosks that are privately owned and operated by SWEs. The majority of residents (70 per cent) collect water from the kiosks, while 16 per cent buy from tertiary SWEs (bicycle/back loaders) who deliver water directly to their households. The kiosk operators consider tertiary SWEs an important component in sustaining their livelihoods.

The major constraints experienced by SWEs include lack of recognition by the relevant authorities, inadequate capital base, high operating costs, and obscure procedures for obtaining a licence or connection.

The greatest opportunity is the existence of the huge market for SWEs to deliver water in Maili Saba and other informal settlements. The positive political climate that currently exists is likely to influence the utility to engage in dialogue with residents in informal settlements to improve water services. Kiosks will continue to play a significant role in the immediate and long-term water services in the informal settlements. Improved relationships between the utility and SWEs will ensure a stable and predictable working environment for SWEs, while at the same time offering the utility a way to provide suitable water delivery services in the short term. The long-term objective will be improved piped distribution networks in the informal settlements, provided directly by the utility.

The primary purpose of this research is to ensure better access by users to affordable and appropriate levels of service. Consumers are an important and key stakeholder in the whole chain. SWEs are important in so far as they provide the water services to consumers, without whom the SWE would not exist. The main user of SWE services in Maili Saba is the household. The consumer's views on SWEs are shaped largely by their understanding of the context of water delivery into informal settlements and therefore they concede that SWEs are important and necessary in the water supply chain. The SWEs provide the necessary capital and infrastructure that makes water available in the settlement and the reliability of the water supply is of crucial importance as it stabilizes people's water bills.

The residents in Maili Saba consider SWEs to be an integral component of their way of life. It is worth noting that the residents considered the cost of water reasonable except in times of shortages. The residents believe that some of these shortages are created in order to push up the price of water. To prevent this from happening the residents consider improved reliability to be the highest priority, and even when they consider community management as an option, the driving force is to improve reliability and thus increase water availability and stabilize prices. It is conceivable that the introduction of community-managed kiosks will distribute their benefits to a large proportion of the population.

The utility

The Nairobi City Water and Sewerage Company's activities are beneficial to the utility because they are reducing water losses and increasing revenue. However, the activities are commercial and they need to inject a service dimension in order to benefit the users. These activities benefit the SWEs as they are seen to be working formally with the utility and this forms a basis on which further work can be built to achieve full legal recognition for SWEs as agents of the utility, and thus help streamline and improve water services in the informal settlements. This pilot project by the utility in Mukuru presents an excellent opportunity for Phase 2 of this research project.

Conclusion

It was observed that SWEs, especially the kiosks, consider water vending a major livelihood/economic activity. Many of the vendors have spent more than five years in this business, suggesting that water vending is a good job that gives the vendors a sustainable livelihood. Water vending supplies up to 60 per cent of Nairobi's population with water. It therefore makes sense to try to create a win–win solution, which helps the SWEs improve the service they offer, reduces the losses suffered by the utility, and provides a better deal to residents. If this were possible, it would represent a major step forwards in improving access to water for millions of the city's poorest people.

Way forward

The current scenario offers opportunities for Phase 2 of the project to pilot, develop and implement the interventions assessed as being the most likely to succeed. The interventions will seek to improve water services for the residents of the informal settlement (Mukuru) where the utility is undertaking a pilot intervention.

Practical Action East Africa (formerly ITDG–EA) will partner with WEDC and the utility to pilot the most feasible interventions.

The most feasible interventions include:

1. **Physical improvements:** To pilot and test a piped distribution system that takes water from the current utility meter chambers into the informal settlement. The improved system will provide meter chambers within the settlement and will be managed by the SWEs. The SWEs will work with the consumers to plan a water pipe route that will provide the most advantages

to both SWEs and users. This pilot will include the provision of bulk meters at the current utility meter chamber and also individual meters within the settlement chamber. This will assist in monitoring water losses that might occur in the pipelines.

The improved reticulation will have the following benefits:

- Water supply in the informal settlement will be improved.

- The utility will have an opportunity to test both management and physical improvement models in informal settlements.

- There is an opportunity for SWEs and users to engage in a joint or shared vision for improving water supply in the settlement.

2. **Strengthening the SWEs:** Phase 2 of the project will develop, test and pilot organizing the SWEs into cooperatives in order to engage with the utility with one voice. The SWEs will be encouraged and supported to form cooperative societies that will engage with the utility and other stakeholders.

   This will also provide the SWEs with an opportunity to seek and receive credit from formal lending institutions. The utility will also be encouraged to pilot financing mechanism where it provides materials to the SWEs and recovers their costs back from sales of water.

3. **Capacity building:** The utility will receive support to document and systematize lesson learning from its current interventions and also from the Phase 2 inputs.

4. **User organization:** The primary purpose of this input is to support attitude change to reduce vandalism and encourage positive dialogue with users and other stakeholders.

The current water sector reforms offer ample opportunity for positive engagement and lesson learning that can stimulate improvements in the way that the utility operates. The lessons will also provide evidence for policy dialogue, as it is a policy that is being put into operation in Kenya and in the region.

Chapter 1

Introduction

1.1 Background

Twenty per cent of Kenya's population of 31 million live in urban centres, 3 million in Nairobi alone. Current estimates show that 60 per cent – or 1.8 million – of Nairobi's residents live in informal settlements, which are characterized by poor basic services such as water, sanitation and shelter. This study focuses on the issues of water provision in the informal settlements of Nairobi, using the Maili Saba informal settlement as a case study.

The primary theme of the study was to investigate the constraints to and opportunities for small water enterprises (SWEs) to play a more significant role in water provision, and what strategies could support them to improve access to water services by low-income residents of urban informal settlements. The primary data was collected in Maili Saba, and interviews were held with officials from the utility and central and local government. Secondary information comes from an extensive literature review carried out at the onset of the project. The research is funded by the UK Department for International Development (DFID) and is being carried out by the Water, Engineering and Development Centre (WEDC) at Loughborough University, UK. The local partner for the research is Practical Action – East Africa (formerly ITDG – East Africa).

1.2 Study goal and purpose

The project goal and purpose for this research, as specified in the project's logframe, are as follows:

Goal

To improve the well-being of the poor in informal urban settlements through cost-effect improvements to water supply services.

Purpose

To identify and test constraints, opportunities and strategies for enabling small water enterprises to deliver acceptable water services to poor urban consumers.

1.3   Research process

The research process has three distinct but inter-related phases:

The Inception Phase included a literature study and a project planning workshop in Nairobi in July 2002. The major documents from the Inception Phase include the project Planning Workshop Report (August 2002) and the Inception Report (December 2002). The Inception Phase considered and clarified a number of different areas of the project. It clarified the geographical focus, the key partners/ stakeholders, and the key components to be addressed in the next phases.

Phase 1 of the research is the subject of the current report. It aimed to develop a contextual understanding and to analyse location. It also aimed to identify, assess and select interventions to improve the performance of SWEs for Phase 2, to begin to build a more favourable environment through contacts with the utilities and other relevant agencies.

Phase 2 will conduct action research to pilot, develop and implement at least two of the interventions assessed as being the most likely to succeed. These interventions will seek to improve water services for the urban poor who rely on SWEs for delivery of water. SWEs will be motivated to take up these new opportunities. Utilities will be encouraged to recognize the potential of engaging with SWEs in order to provide water services to those customers not currently served by the utility's distribution system by working with SWEs.

1.4   Research issues

Drawing from the goal, purpose and the contextual understanding developed in the Inception Phase, the following overarching research issues were identified for Phase 1.

- How do different groups of poor people in urban informal settlements currently obtain access to water services and what are their (major) remaining needs?

- What incentives and constraints exist that will affect the ability of SWEs to improve the water services they provide to the poor?

- What constraints exist (and what opportunities might exist) that will affect utilities' ability to engage with SWEs to improve services to users within informal urban settlements?

- What are the key obstacles that block collaboration between utilities and SWEs in informal urban settlements, and how might they be overcome?

- What are appropriate improvements to service standards and how can they be secured?

- How can others benefits from the lessons learned from successful interventions be used to improve services to users?

1.5   Methodology

The research method was carefully selected to achieve the above research objectives. Due to the complexity of the issues, the significance of context and lack of existing work in this area, a case study methodology was found to be the most appropriate research technique for contextual studies of Phase 1. Within the case study methodology, qualitative techniques were used in order to capture the perspectives of various stakeholders relevant to the study.

The major steps in the research were a literature review that included local 'grey' literature to ensure that the best use was made of existing information. Semi-structured interviews were conducted using pre-tested questionnaires and checklists. Focus group discussions were conducted with consumer groups and by gender. Researchers undertook intensive individual interviews with carefully selected informants and conducted participant observation and settlement walks.

1.6   Stakeholder analysis

Four key stakeholders were identified:
- Small water enterprises (SWEs)

- Users

- Water utilities

- Public agencies

The project seeks ways to enable small water enterprises (SWEs) to deliver a better service to poor consumers in informal settlements by encouraging better collaboration and partnership with water utilities. It is believed that interventions to improve the performance of SWEs can be identified from a synthesis of the findings from the four research dimensions, in particular, the convergence between the constraints/opportunities identified for SWEs, the institutional and policy levers identified for the utilities, and the prioritizing of interventions that address the needs and preferences of the users.

1.7   Literature review

Background

The literature review shows that the Kenyan government has initiated major reforms in water service delivery. The publication of Sessional Paper No.1 of 1999 on 'Water Resources Management' was the first major government initiative in improving water resources management. The Sessional Paper describes the government's concrete objectives for efficient water resources management. Further to that, the government published the 'Water Act 2002' that introduces major reforms in the water sector. The Act provides for the creation of the Water Resources Management Authority, Water Services Regulatory Board, Water Services Board, Water Services Providers, and Water Services Trust Fund. The Act limits the role of the government in water resources management to policy direction and supervision, and strengthens the role of public and private sector providers.

In the case of Nairobi, small water enterprises complement the city council in the informal settlements by reaching consumers who are not served by the council. The water kiosk and standpipe's share of the market is between 75 and 90 per cent of the water demand in low-income areas. In the case of Kibera informal settlement, individual residents who are both vendors and end-users of the kiosks predominantly own their water kiosks. Many kiosks are operated as family enterprises alongside other small-scale businesses and serve a dual role – as a source of income and source of water for domestic use. On average, each kiosk sells about 50 jerrycans of water a day. Individuals own and operate 98 per cent of the kiosks and self-help and other community groups operate the other 2 per cent.

Nairobi City Council has performed poorly in the management of the water supply system. The amount of water the council supplies to the informal settlement is unknown; billings are sporadic, irregular, not based on volumes used, and cover 30 per cent of customers. Only about 13 per cent of the billed amount is collected. In effect, the Water and Sewerage Department (WSD) provides water to owners of kiosks and individual connections who on-sell the water and pocket the cash. During shortages people often spend two to four hours collecting water and prices shoot up to two to five times their normal value, to KSh5–30 per 20-litre jerrycan.

The sustainable livelihoods approach recognizes that households need access to assets so as to provide for their basic needs and for the need to gradually build up their assets over time. Such assets include properly planned physical infrastructure, particularly roads, water and markets (Syagga, 2001). The access to, use of, and interaction among the assets serve as a foundation for a livelihood system and this requires a deliberate targeted enabling strategy for the very poor.

Water kiosks in Nairobi's informal settlements are either owned by individual operators or, in a few cases, by community-based organizations (CBOs). For some years now the city council, the supplier of water, has relaxed connection procedures for applicants within informal settlements and no longer insists on title deeds or a lease as proof of land ownership before agreeing a connection (Bosire, 2002).

The relaxation in requirements for water connections in informal settlements in Nairobi was effected through a council resolution, which also exempted the water retailers from paying the council bulk rate and allowed them to pay the normal rate applicable to other individual residential users. The 1974 water by-laws have not been relaxed, so still remain the same, and need to be reviewed to bring them in line with the council resolution. The relaxation in Nairobi City Council water policy to allow for water connections in informal settlements, though it results in water availability in these areas, raises the following efficacy and sustainability concerns:

- A lot of water goes to waste due to poor workmanship, inadequate supervision by city council staff during construction, and use of poor quality pipes (e.g. using electrical ducts instead of water pipes). In most cases the water consumed is also contaminated by leakages.

- Bill collection from these areas by the city council is said to be less than 5 per cent. Although the poor end-users pay the operators at a higher unit rate than the council charges the operators, the operators do not pay the council, and so pocket the entire fee.

- The need for the chief and area councillor to identify each applicant and support their application for water connection more often than not ends up as a 'gate keeping' cost, which not only increases connection costs for water vendors, but also ends up being passed on to the end-users.

- The high retail prices charged (an average of KSh2 per 20-litre container) means that large numbers of informal settlement residents cannot afford to purchase sufficient potable water for their needs and resort to unsatisfactory alternative sources, such as the highly contaminated Nairobi River and roof water catchment, which may be polluted by dirt on the collection surface (Bosire, 2002).

The role of various actors in Kenya's water sector

Albu and Njiru (2002) make a useful distinction between wholesale vendors (who may buy a tanker or even have a small network), distributing vendors (who sell directly to consumers door-to-door), and direct vendors (who sell to consumers who come to them).

The way in which privatization, in Kenya and elsewhere, is carried out indicates that the underlying aim is commercial rather than service-oriented.

Business and Economics Research (BER, 1999) proposes a partnership between the Water and Sewerage Department and the Kibera community in the management of water suppliers. It suggests that:

- All account holders (kiosk operators and holders of private connections) in a village form and join a legally registered Village Water Sellers Association (VWSA or cooperative).

- The VWSA (or cooperative) buys water, in bulk, from the Water and Sewerage Department, replacing the current individual interaction between department officials and each account holder.

- Members of the VWSA or cooperative purchase water from the VWSA.

- All the members (account holders) of the VWSA or cooperative are allowed to sell water.

- All members of the VWSA or cooperative sell the water to end-users as at present.

- The price of water at each level of transaction allows for recovery of best practice costs pertaining to that level.

- Water transactions at all levels should be on the basis of pre-payments or payment at the moment of withdrawal.

- Unhindered competition between kiosk owners is encouraged to become the hallmark for the pricing of water to consumers (BER, 1999).

Constraints

Only one out of every six kiosks had any form of physical 'superstructure'. A number of kiosks are operated from windows of shops. There was little or no provision for waste disposal, resulting in stagnant pools of water within the settlement. Wastewater was, however, being better managed among kiosks owned by individuals than by self-help groups (Kariuki et al., 2000). In general kiosk owners:

- depend on the utility sector infrastructure services;

- do not market enough or advertise their services;

- have no formal training in their operations;

- lack information on training needs and opportunities; and

- lack the sound financial base required to finance their business operations (Njoroge and Obel-Lawson, 2000:5).

Njoroge and Obel-Lawson (2000) recommended the following issues as a follow-up of their Kibera water kiosk study:
- There is a need to strengthen the management skills and capacity of the SWEs, to inform them of available training facilities, and to explore potential financing channels.

- The Nairobi City Council and other authorities should introduce the SWEs to the communities. Hygiene awareness should be promoted to the urban poor (Njoroge and Obel-Lawson, 2000:6).

In Mombasa and Nairobi land tenure policy is unclear as informal settlements are considered illegal. Investors are therefore unwilling to support the provision and improvement of basic social services and infrastructure in the low-income areas (Obel-Lawson and Njoroge, 2000:2).

Success factors of small water enterprises (SWEs)

- SWEs thrive due to the inability of the monopolistic enterprises to respond to the dynamics of market demand.

- They are able to access (physically) peri-urban areas not covered by the public sector enterprises.

- They are commercially oriented operations based on private enterprise and designed to make money (the profit motive compels innovative approaches to resolution of difficulties, which in turn ensures sustainability of service).

- SWEs respond to the needs of the market by accessing high-density communities by providing standpipes and water kiosks.

- They operate other businesses in addition to providing water services (this permits re-allocation of resources whenever necessary to keep the entire group of enterprises working).

Other constraints

- The poor infrastructure in informal, low-income settlements limits SWEs' ability to access their customers.

- Poverty limits the viability of investments in most of the needy areas.

- Poor construction standards applied in some of the public facilities have caused problems in terms of both the development and maintenance needed to handle a growing population.

- Poor law enforcement in the urban environmental services sector, coupled with an inadequate legal framework (for Dar es Salaam, Kampala and Mombasa) frustrates the good job done by SWEs.

- The low literacy level among the urban poor makes them slow to adjust to new ideas from SWEs.

- The taxation system favours utilities, creating negative feelings in the private sector. This results in poor bookkeeping, no auditing, and evasion of taxes by SWEs.

- There is poor access to credit due to the lack of information about the existence of appropriate private sector development programmes.

Case study: Key characteristics of Nairobi Water kiosks

- These facilities are totally reliant on Nairobi City Council bulk supply.

- Their major advantage is that tankers cannot access the informal settlements as the poor road infrastructure prevents bigger mobile operators from entering the market.

- Their set-up costs are relatively low.

- Nairobi City Council is unable to efficiently collect water bills and this lowers the cost of bulk water supply to the kiosk operators.

- They charge between US$0.02 and US$0.05 for a 20-litre container, and most kiosks sell about 300 litres of water a day. Thus, daily water kiosk sales average between US$0.3 and US$0.75.

Families would normally operate the kiosks, which are either attached or near their residence. This brings down labour costs and, in some instances, there are no real costs (World Bank, 2000:12).

Policy impacts on small-scale urban water provision in Kenya

The legal issues touching on the water sector are supposed to be contained in the Water Act 2002. There are, however, a total of twenty-six other Acts of Parliament which have a bearing on issues concerning water, for example the Local Government Act, Public Health Act and Environmental Management and Co-ordination Act.

Operation and maintenance of water supplies has recently become one of the major problems in the water sector. This has been mainly due to a multiplicity of factors touching on planning, design, implementation and operation and maintenance. This has resulted in water supply systems that have become unsustainable in terms of operation and maintenance. In line with government policy on cost sharing, the ministry in charge of water affairs will fully encourage the active participation of beneficiaries in the development and operation of water supplies. In this regard, the government will continue to promote the development of water systems that are self-sustaining and where the beneficiaries are encouraged to take the full responsibility for operating and maintaining such systems. To ensure controlled withdrawal mechanisms, the government will undertake to train the communities on issues related to the operation and maintenance of water projects and have them assume the management of the projects systematically to prevent disruption of services (GoK, 1999:38–9).

There are many organizations involved in water resource management and the development of water supplies in Kenya. These organizations include the Ministry of Water Resources Management and Development, state corporations, local authorities and private organizations. These organizations have not been very successful in managing water affairs because of some institutional weaknesses, which have been identified and include poor organizational structure, inadequate funds, lack of skilled personnel, and shortage of essential facilities (GoK, 1999:41).

The current debate on urban water management

UN-HABITAT (2003:67) provides indicative per capita consumption rates for a sample of cities in developing economies. In Accra, in the expensive residential areas with piped household water supplies and flush toilets for sanitation, water consumption per capita is well in excess of the recommended 200 litres per person per day. In Accra's slum neighbourhoods, such as Nima-Maamobi and Ashiaman, where buying water from vendors is common, water consumption is about 60 litres per person per day. In Dar es Salaam, average daily per person water consumption is 164 litres, but it is as low as 44 litres in low-income areas. In Nairobi, average daily water consumption varies between 20 and 200 litres per person, depending on the quality of water provision.

A study of independent water providers in cities of ten African nations highlighted the variety of providers, which includes:

- hand-pushed carts that carry 100–200 litres of water;

- horse or donkey-pulled carts with up to 500 litres (especially in cities of the Sahel, where draught animals are raised in abundance);

- water truckers who serve larger customers, for example filling water tanks in larger houses or offices; and

- various types of water resellers operating from fixed points of sale, including standpipe vendors and, in some cities, mini piped networks (Collignon and Vezina, 2000).

In Sub-Saharan Africa, water and sanitation remains the responsibility of central, rather than local, government, in contrast to the situation in for example, Latin America. African governments have presented water and sanitation, along with other community services, as basic public services to which all citizens are entitled, with generous public subsidies as required. In rural areas, this promise has been fulfilled through central government investment in wells and boreholes, generally run at a substantial loss by community associations. In urban areas, however, where public water service is assigned to a single citywide authority, many residents have no direct access to clean piped public water (Collignon and Vezina, 2000:10).

1.8   Structure of this report

This report consists of 11 chapters, plus an Executive Summary. The research process and main objectives are given in Chapter 1, while the national context and the Nairobi situation are covered in Chapters 2 and 3 respectively.

The current sector issues, highlighting the sector reforms, SWEs in the setting of private sector participation, and the MDGs are covered in Chapter 4.

Chapter 5 describes Maili Saba, the research location, while Chapter 6 links poverty with water services. The main focus for Chapter 7 is SWEs, the value chain, and opportunities and constraints. Chapters 8 and 9 provide the consumer perspective and a description of the relationships between utilities and the SWEs.

The consensus-building workshops are covered in Chapter 10, while Chapter 11 gives the conclusions and the recommendations.

The way forward (Phase 2) proposal is in Appendix 1.

Chapter 2

Water Supply in Kenya: The National Context

2.1 A brief history

At independence in 1963 the Government of Kenya (GoK) realized that provision of adequate water was a major factor in promoting economic development. A Water Development Department was formed, which became a fully fledged ministry in 1974. In the 1960s and 70s communities in the spirit of Harambee (or 'self-help') initiated a large number of self-help water projects, alongside the government-initiated ones, and developed rural and urban water supplies (GoK and JICA, 1992:2).

In the period 1974–78 the public sector played a major role in the provision of water services. Consequently, central government took over the self-help (community) and local authority water supplies to operate, manage and maintain. Thus, central government involvement in the water sector overshadowed the self-help and local authorities initiatives. The private sector was involved in design and construction activities. This central government involvement was later to prove too big a financial burden, particularly in the operation and maintenance of all water supplies in the country. Non-governmental organizations' (NGOs') operations have increased, mainly in support of community-based water supplies.

2.2 National water resources

Kenya is classified as a water-scarce country. The current reforms provide an appropriate opportunity to address both the water resources management and the development of water supply systems/services, taking into account the water deficiency and the needs of the population.

The reforms also provide an opportunity to review and recognize the involvement of all stakeholders. SWEs are an integral component of the water supply chain, especially in informal settlements in urban centres.

Drainage systems

The drainage system in Kenya is determined by the Great Rift Valley, which runs roughly north–south, and from its flanks water flows westwards to Lake Victoria and eastwards to the Indian Ocean. From this, Kenya's drainage system is sub-divided into five drainage basins and 192 subdivisions. The five drainage basins are:

(a)   Lake Victoria basin (46,229 km²) comprises the whole of the area west of the Rift Valley that drains into Lake Victoria.

(b)   The Rift Valley basin (130,452 km²) is an area of internal drainage discharging into Lake Turkana in the north and Lake Natron in the south.

(c)   The Athi / Sabaki River basin (66,837 km²) comprises the southern part of the country east of the Rift Valley. It drains the southern slopes of the Aberdare mountain range and the flanks of the Rift Valley south of the Athi River.

(d)   The Tana River basin (126,026 km²) drains the eastern slopes of the Aberdare mountain range, the southern slopes of Mount Kenya, and the Nyambene mountain range and discharges into the Indian Ocean. The Tana is the largest river in Kenya.

(e)   The Ewaso Nyiro / North River basin (210,226 km²) comprises the northern part of Kenya and drains the northern slopes of the Aberdare mountains and Mount Kenya into the Indian Ocean.

Table 2.1.   Major catchment and river basins in Kenya

Catchment area	Area (km²)	Rainfall mm	Runoff flow/year (106 m³)
Lake Victoria	46,021	234	10,769
Rift Valley	124,722	27	3,367
Athi/Sabaki River	66,420	38	2,524
Tana River	126,927	49	6,219
Ewaso Nyiro/ North River	209,320	7	1,465
	Total: 573,410	Weighted average: 42 (= Total runoff ÷ Area)	Total: 24,344

Source: Van Doorne (1985)

Surface water

Surface water occupies about 16,860,000 ha of the country, comprising 1,120,000 ha of inland waters and 1,430,000 ha of Indian Ocean territorial waters. A further 14,310,000 ha includes the exclusive Economic Zone, also part of the Indian Ocean. There are 36 large-scale dams that exist or are under construction, in all the river basins in the country (about 800 including dams of all sizes). Lake Victoria is shared between Kenya, Uganda and Tanzania, and is the second-largest freshwater lake in the world.

Groundwater

In arid and semi-arid lands, the inadequacy and unreliability of water supplies poses the most serious development constraint for agriculture, livestock and other resource development activities. The most substantial groundwater abstraction is through boreholes.

Table 2.2.	Number of boreholes and their uses	
Borehole	**No. of boreholes**	**Percentage of total (%)**
Public water supply	2124	22.7
Agricultural	944	10.1
Domestic	435	4.6
Industrial/commercial	244	2.4
Livestock	176	1.9
Observation	62	0.7
Exploratory	51	0.5
Others	910	9.7
Multiple uses	4,438	47.4
Total	**9,364**	**100.0**

Source: Unpublished data provided by UNDP, Nairobi

2.3   Water supplies

Urban water supply

The Ministry of Water recognizes 103 gazetted towns as urban centres. Some 73 urban centres are served by central government water supplies, 21 by the National Water Conservation and Pipeline Corporation (NWCPC), and nine urban centres by water supplies operated and maintained by the municipal councils. The rest of the small towns and trading centres are considered 'rural' and receive little support for water supplies from central government.

Low-income households account for 30–70 per cent of the urban population, depending upon the city or town, and comprise the fastest growing segment of the urban population. Between 1993 and 2000 the percentage of the total urban population below the absolute poverty line rose from 27 to 49 per cent. Small water enterprises supply more than 60 per cent of the urban poor through water kiosks or vendors. Some slum dwellers get their water from heavily polluted natural water sources (rivers, wells and streams).

Because of the rapid degradation of the public water service, many small water enterprises have been providing a substitute services to all categories of customers. In formal settlements, SWEs typically finance and operate boreholes equipped with mechanized pumps, small distribution networks, and water tankers (6 to 8 m³); they obtain a water abstraction permit, but rarely a water vending licence. In informal settlements, SWEs mainly operate water kiosks or sell small quantities (20-litre jerrycans or 100-litre drums).

Table 2.3.	Average availability of water in urban areas					
Water supply	Population (000s)	Population with household connection	Population with public waterpoint	Population served	Population unserved	Population served %
Urban water	9,957	3,566	2,188	8,662	1,295	87
Rural water	20,123	2,904	6,613	6,238	13,885	31
Total water	30,080	61470	8,801	14,900	15,180	49

Source: Unpublished data provided by UNDP, Nairobi

Rural water supply

It is estimated that between 30 and 50 per cent of the rural population have access to an improved water supply through piped and point source systems. Community water supplies run on a self-help basis serve about 2.3 million people in urban areas and 2.6 million people in rural areas. These self-help groups are normally registered with the Department of Culture and Social Services, but this kind of registration does not provide the groups with the necessary legal status to protect their roles/rights. Thus these systems are extremely vulnerable to manipulation and mismanagement including vandalism and political and economic manipulation.

Natural and traditional water sources, though often polluted, provide significant alternative water sources in the rural areas.

Arid and semi-arid lands (ASAL)
The main constraint to development, income generation and food security in the ASAL areas is inadequate water supplies. The government has identified dams, water pans, and boreholes as the most appropriate options to supply water to these areas. The priority is the rehabilitation and construction of these facilities in partnership with local communities and with support from bilateral and multilateral agencies.

Master plans
A joint Government of Kenya – Government of Sweden study was conducted between 1976 and 1981 to develop a national water master plan. This was later updated through the second national water master plan study, carried out between 1990 and 1992. These two studies, in addition to proposing a framework for future development, highlighted the major problems and constraints in the sector, among which was the lack of a comprehensive policy/institutional/legal frameworks to guide water sector development (GoK, 1999:3–4). Currently (2003–4) the Ministry of Water is updating the National Water Master Plan using a grant from the International Development and Research Corporation (IDRC) of Canada.

2.4   Current sector issues

Water sector reforms
GoK initiated major reforms in the water sector when it published Sessional Paper No.1 of 1999 on Water Resources Management. The Sessional Paper presents the government's concrete objectives to tackle the main obstacle to efficient water supply and resources management. Building on the recommendations of Sessional Paper No.1, the government published the Water Act 2002, which provides an opportunity for major reforms in the water sector.

Legal/regulatory arrangements
The legal issues pertaining to the water sector are contained in the Water Act 2002. There are, however, a total of twenty-six other acts of parliament which have a bearing on water issues, for example Local Government Act, Public Health Act and Environmental Management and Co-ordination Act. None of these laws recognizes the role of the SWEs in the water supply chain.

Institutional arrangements

The water sector reform process in Kenya is in progress and is said to be about 70 per cent complete. The key institutions being put in place are shown in Figure 2.1.

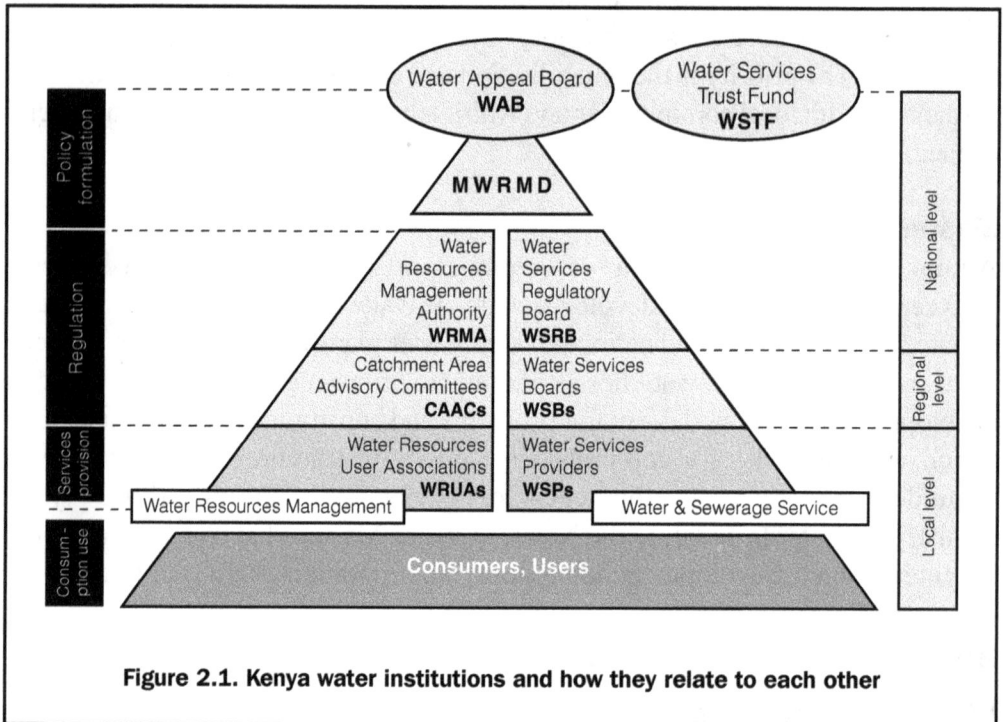

Figure 2.1. Kenya water institutions and how they relate to each other

Source: WSRS

The Ministry of Water and Irrigation

The roles of the ministry are as follows:

- Water catchment conservation, control and protection
- Water resources management policy
- Water apportionment policy
- Water quality and pollution control
- Rural water development and supply
- Urban water development and supply
- Wastewater treatment

- Flood control and land reclamation

- Irrigation and dam construction

- Water Resources Management Authority

- Water Services Regulatory Board

- Water Services Boards

- Water Trust Fund

- National Water Conservation & Pipeline Corporation

- National Irrigation Board

- Kenya Water Institutes

- Water Appeal Board

Water Resource Management Authority

The Water Act 2002 Section 7–8 creates the Water Resources Management Authority, which is in charge of the management and use of water resources. The Authority has the following powers and functions:

(a) To develop principles, guidelines and procedures for the allocation of water resources.

(b) To monitor, and from time to time re-assess, the national water resources management strategy.

(c) To receive and determine applications for permits for water use.

(d) To monitor and enforce conditions attached to permits for water use.

(e) To regulate and protect water resource quality from adverse impacts.

(f) To manage and protect water catchments.

(g) In accordance with guidelines in the water resources management strategy, to determine charges to be imposed for the use of water from any source.

(h) To gather and maintain information on water resources and from time to time to publish forecasts, projections and information on water resources.

(i) To liaise with other bodies for the better regulation and management of water resources.

(j) To advise the Minister concerning any matter in connection with water resources.

Water Service Boards

Section 53 of the Act defines the powers and function of Water Services Boards. A Water Services Board shall, as a licensee, be responsible for the efficient economical provision of water services authorized by the licence. Sections 51–55 of the Act create Water Services Boards and Water Service Providers. Water Services Boards may arrange for the exercise and performance of all or any of its powers and functions under licence to one or more agents, to be known as water service providers. Section 55, Sub-section (3) of the Act demands that the agreement shall specify the powers and functions under the licence, which shall be exercised and performed by the water service provider during the currency of the agreement.

Water Service Providers

Sub-section (5) states that the Water Services Board may enter into agreements with more than one water service provider in respect of its area of supply. Section 56 (1) states that no person shall, on provision of water within the limits of supply of a licensee:

- provide water services to more than twenty households; or

- supply:

  - more than 25,000 litres of water a day for domestic purposes; or

  - more than 100,000 litres of water a day for any purpose, except under authority of the licence.

The Nairobi Water Service Board has licensed the Nairobi City Water and Sewerage Company as the water provider for the City of Nairobi. The Service Board is responsible for the neighbouring districts including Kiambu, Thika, Kajiado, and Machakos, among others, while the company is responsible for the area covered by the City of Nairobi. The water sources harnessed by the company lie outside the boundaries of the city.

Water Service Trust Fund

Section 83 creates the Water Services Trust Fund. The object of the Fund is to assist in financing the provision of water services to areas of Kenya that are without adequate water services. The fund shall receive designated funds directly from Parliament. Funding may come from various sources, including donations, grants, and bequests.

The Government of Kenya, in 'Economic Recovery Strategy for Wealth Creation and Employment Creation' (2003b), details the previous initiatives in water management and reiterates government's commitment to improve water and sanitation services. The government proposes to undertake comprehensive institutional reforms that will facilitate measures to reduce poverty through water and sanitation services programmes.

Box 2.1. Key elements of water sector reforms in Kenya

The water sector reforms are being implemented and the following bodies and processes are being established:

- Water Services Regulatory Board (overall water resources management and regulation)
- Water Services Boards (provision of water and sanitation services, asset development)
- Government to transfer existing water and sanitation schemes to Service Boards, communities and other lower level actors
- Involvement of private sector participation in financing and management of services
- Development of models for distribution of water and sanitation to the poor
- Water Services Trust Fund to facilitate financing of water and sanitation services
- Role of central government in the sector limited to policy/legal and institutional issues

---

Water policy

Current government policy is to withdraw from direct implementation and management of water schemes. Existing schemes will be handed over to communities, local authorities and other service providers. These water schemes will be rehabilitated and the capacities of the communities and local authorities strengthened before the schemes are handed over to them. This will be achieved by developing a rehabilitation programme with the stakeholders to enhance ownership and facilitate choice of technologies (for new schemes) that are appropriate for management by communities and the other service providers. Handing over also requires clearly defined mechanisms to guide the process, and a functional legal and institutional framework.

For urban water utilities, the proposal is to involve the private sector in financing and managing the water supply services. Although investments in urban utilities have been substantial, the poor have received little attention in the planning process and access remains very low. The strategy proposes a sharp focus on peri-urban areas by developing models for distribution and management of water supply and sanitation services and expansion of infrastructure.

Chapter 3

Water Supply Situation in Nairobi

3.1   A brief history

Nairobi's water supply and distribution system has been expanded periodically in order to meet the city's growing water demands. In 1984 the water supply was increased from 130,000 to 190,000 m^3/d, and further increased in 1995 to 400,000 m^3/day with a potential for 519,000 m^3/d. Current water production is 364,000 m^3/d. The bulk water supply to the city is approximately 120 litres per person per day, and about 51 per cent of the bulk water is lost through leakage due to both the poor state of the reticulation system and illegal connections. Billing and revenue collection is very poor, causing the utility financial difficulties.

In 1989 Nairobi City Council embarked on studies to reduce the level of unaccounted-for water and especially leakage by instituting a Leakage Control Programme. Activities included bulk-metering, assessment of data from the metering system, pilot investigations in leakage control methods, and formulation of a leakage control policy. A Leakage Control Section within the Water and Sewerage Department was subsequently established. Despite support by external consultants and financiers, the programme did not realize sustainable results.

3.2   Institutional arrangements

The Nairobi City Water and Sewerage Company Limited (NWSC), a company wholly owned by the Nairobi City Council, has replaced the Department of Water and Sewerage. The new company, which is set to operate autonomously under the Companies Act, is the official water provider for the city of Nairobi. The company buys bulk water from the Nairobi Water Services Board and sells it to consumers through metered outlets.

During the past 10 months, the NWSC has embarked on an innovative approach to reduce unaccounted-for water and increase revenue through an Informal Settlements Projects. This project is working in 15 informal settlements and aims to identify and regularize existing illegal /quasi-legal connections in the informal settlements by providing a lockable meter chamber in the vicinity of the informal settlements and registering and then billing all these connections. Where in the past leakages due to poor workmanship and poor quality pipes caused unaccounted-for water, the current approach ensures that the meters are all at the point of connection to the water mains, so the poor workmanship or pipe materials that cause leakages occur after the meter – effectively transferring all the losses to the SWEs in the informal settlements. Disconnections are also easy to effect, as the meters are outside the settlements and easily accessible. This improvement may mean increased water charges at the kiosks as the SWEs seek to retain their current profit margins even though they now have to cope with water losses and the cost of laying new pipes (as current chamber positions may not always correspond to existing take-off points for the SWEs).

The majority of these metered connections are made for SWEs who sell water to end-users. The distances between the meter chambers and the individual kiosks vary from between 50 and 800 metres. The vendors (kiosk owners) are not organized and deal individually with both the utility and with the users (their customers). The users have little influence on the retail price of the water and continue to pay between KSh2 and KSh3 per 20 litres of water.

3.3   Legal and regulatory framework

The Water Act 2002 is the principal legislation that governs all the activities of the water sector. The Local Governments Act establishes local authorities that can enact by-laws specific to their needs. The water tariffs are governed by the Water Act. The current water tariff in Nairobi City Council is progressive, starting with KSh12 per m^3 for the first 10 m^3.

Residents of slum/informal settlements do not receive water (officially) from the Nairobi water supply as the settlements are considered illegal and temporary – despite many of them being as old as the city itself or even older. Current efforts by the company are changing this landscape by piloting metered connections at a central point adjacent to the informal settlements. There is no direct interaction between the utility and the kiosk customers.

3.4   Water resources

Nairobi's main water supply is from surface sources in different locations at difference places.

These sources and their daily production are shown in Table 3.1.

Table 3.1. Principal water sources for the city of Nairobi	
Source	Volume (m³/day)
Kikuyu Springs	4,000
Sasumua Dam	43,000
Ruiru Dam	12,000
Ng'ethu	305,000
Total	364,000

Source: Howard Humphreys (Kenya) Ltd, 1996

The Kabete treatment plant receives water from the Sasumua Dam, Ruiru Dam and Kikuyu Springs. The Gigiri water system, developed in phases, receives water from Ng'ethu Water Treatment Plant. The Gigiri Water Supply System includes the Middle Chania pumping station and Mwagu intake. Most of these intakes and treatment plants are between 50 and 150 km away from Nairobi.

3.5   Water infrastructure

Transmission

The main water transmission system includes the raw water mains from the sources to the treatment works, the transmission of treated water from the treatment works to the various reservoirs in the supply areas, and the transfer lines through which water is pumped from one reservoir to another.

Sasumua to Kabete: A single 900 mm raw water main under the dam bifurcates into 675 mm and 400 mm steel pipes to the treatment works. After treatment, twin pipes of varying diameters extend to as far as the Ruiru Junction, where they join as a single pipe to Kabete. The design capacity of this transmission system is 193,000 m³/d and it operates at a measured capacity of 172,300 m³/d (89 per cent efficiency).

Ruiru to Kabete: Four steel mains (400 mm, 300 mm, 300 mm and 225 mm) take raw water from Ruiru Dam to Ruiru Junction where the two 300 mm mains join. From here, three mains (400 mm, 300 mm and 225 mm) take water to the Kabete treatment works. The capacity of this transmission system is 30,050 m³/d and it operates at 26,780 m³ when boosted and 24,190 m³ under gravity.

Mwagu intake to Ng'ethu: The raw water transmission system between Mwagu and Ng'ethu treatment works is part tunnel and part pipeline. From the intake, a tunnel 2.7 km long leads to an outlet portal in the Mataara River valley. Twin steel raw water mains of 1200 and 1400 mm diameter transfer water from the Mataara tunnel to Ng'ethu Water treatment works.

Table 3.2. Mwangu intake to Ng'ethu transmission system		
Element	**Capacity (m³/day)**	
	Design	**Measured**
Mwagu intake	460,000	460,000
Mataara tunnel	230,000†	460,000
Raw water mains	270,000	265,000
	195,000	-

† Original design assumed tunnel operating half full, but it can achieve the measured capacity at maximum flow.

Thika Dam to Chania River: The intake of the Thika Dam discharges raw water through a submerged discharge valve into a 2.5 m diameter horseshoe tunnel that is 1 km long. The tunnel discharges into a tributary of the Kiama River just upstream of its confluence with the main river. Approximately 450 m downstream a small concrete weir diverts the flow into a second tunnel. This horseshoe tunnel, 3.4 km long and 2.5 m in diameter, takes water from the Kiama to the Chania River where water discharges into the river via a man-made waterfall.

Table 3.3. Thika Dam to Chania River system	
Tunnel section	**Design capacity (m³/day)**
Thika to Kiama	460,000
Kiama to Kimakia	500,000
Kimakia to Chania	540,000

Source: Howard Humphreys (Kenya) Ltd, 1996

Ng'ethu to Gigiri: The treated-water transmission system has been developed in three phases, as shown in Table 3.4.

Table 3.4. Ng'ethu to Gigiri transmission system development		
Phase	**Capacity (m³/day)**	
	Design	**Measured**
1	49,600	48,800
2	128,000	128,000
3	863,000	-

Source: Howard Humphreys (Kenya) Ltd, 1996

The main pumped transfers lines within the city system are shown in Table 3.5.

Table 3.5. Main pumped transfer lines		
Pumping line		
From	**To**	**Capacity (m³/d)**
Kabete	Dagoretti	15,800
Kabete	Uthiru	16,500
Gigiri	Kabete	46,000
Kyuna	Loresho Tower	2,600
Kenyatta Avenue	Hill tank	17,500

Source: Howard Humphreys (Kenya) Ltd, 1996

Storage capacities

The various reservoirs that supply Nairobi City Council are, where possible, located where they can conveniently feed their relevant areas using only gravity pressure. They are part of two distribution systems, the Kabete and Gigiri systems.

Table 3.6.	Existing water reservoir storage capacities	
Distribution system	**Service reservoir**	**Capacity (m³)**
Kabete	Dagoretti Forest	11,000
	Uthiru	11,000
	Loresho Water Tower	450
	Kabete	99,000
	Hill Tank	18,000
	Kikuyu Tanks	2,000
	Kyuna / Loresho	9,000
Gigiri	Gigiri	79,900
	Kiambu	44,000
	Karura	9,450
	Wilson	9,000
	Ring Road Tower	450
	Kasarani	44,000

Source: Howard Humphreys (Kenya) Ltd, 1996

Distribution system

Most of the areas served by the distribution systems are supplied from the distribution lines fed by the water reservoirs. The supply areas fed from the Kabete system are divided into two: the upper and middle supply areas. The upper supply area is served by reservoirs at Dagoretti and Uthiru, and the Loresho Water Tower. The middle supply area is fed by gravity from the Kyuna and Kabete reservoirs and Hill tank. The rest of the Nairobi (lower) supply area is fed by gravity from the Gigiri water supply system.

3.6 Coverage and demand

Nairobi has experienced rapid population growth and industrial expansion without a corresponding infrastructure development to meet the demand for water. Official 1998 statistics from the Central Bureau of Statistics indicate that 96.9 per cent of non-poor households and 93.3 per cent of poor households have access to safe drinking water. According to the Ministry of Finance and Planning (GoK, 2000b), safe water is defined as piped water in the compound, water from a public outdoor tap/borehole, or water from protected wells. Unsafe water is defined as unprotected well/rainwater, lake/river/pond water, water supplied by vendors or trucks, and water from other sources. Nairobi City Council supplies account for 93 per cent of all the water consumed in Nairobi, and the table below shows water demand projections. Water supplied by vendors is considered to be 'unimproved', because of its variable quality. Water purchased from kiosks is, however, considered to be from an improved source, because it is from a piped supply at the point of delivery to the customer.

Table 3.7. Water demand projections for Nairobi		
Year	Demand ('000 m³/day)	Average growth % per year
1985	203	
1995	287	3.5
2010	447	3.0

Source: Njoroge and Obel-Lawson, 2000

If all the bulk water produced were delivered, it would provide 120 litres per person per day. However, water losses reduce bulk availability by at least 50 per cent, thus making it difficult to meet the demand for clean safe drinking water (Njoroge and Obel-Lawson, 2000). According to a survey conducted by the company Seureca in 1998 of Nairobi's 1,980,000 people, 929,000 have utility connections and 1,000,000 obtain water from secondary sources, mainly through SWEs. (Note that population data for Nairobi can vary greatly, depending on how population figures are obtained. The population of informal settlements is very fluid, and many people move in to Nairobi from rural areas.) The same source estimates that in January 1997, 239,000 m³ of water was used daily and water use was 60 per cent for domestic uses, 32 per cent for commercial /institutional uses, and 8 per cent for industrial use. The current water situation in Nairobi is aggravated by huge water losses, despite the fact that the water is being transported long distances which ought to call for stringent control measures to curb waste and leakages.

3.7   Conclusion

Nairobi's institutional arrangements have been reorganized to introduce the new Nairobi City Water and Sewerage Company, which has been licensed by the Nairobi Water Service Board as the water provider for Nairobi. The company has embarked on a pilot scheme to reduce water losses and increase revenue by providing water meter chambers from which to connect the SWEs serving the informal settlements.

The current bulk water supply is able to provide 120 litres per person per day, which is approximately 60 per cent of the recommended daily consumption. The 50 per cent losses reduce considerably the water available to consumers, however, while denying the utility much-needed revenue. The bulk water sources are a long way away from the city, necessitating huge and expensive transmission networks. As water demands in the vicinity of the bulk water sources are likely to increase in future, conservation and prudent water use in the city will become increasingly necessary.

Chapter 4

Current Sector Issues

In this chapter, we will consider some of the details of the water sector reforms, the situation of SWEs in light of private sector participation in the water sector, and issues of land tenure (as this is a major hindrance for the utilities in providing services to the informal settlements). We will also consider the Millennium Development Goals, as they provide a statement of intent to reduce by half un-served populations, most of whom reside in informal settlements. Also of interest are incentives to serve the poor (including by increasing political goodwill), focusing on gender (especially the poor women who bear the brunt of the problems of poor water services delivery in already constrained household budgets), and population growth in the city, as most people end up in poor but affordable accommodation in the informal settlements. SWEs are a major player in the provision of services in informal settlements.

4.1   Water sector reforms

The current water sector reforms are built on the national water and sanitation policy (Sessional Paper No.1 of 1999) and embedded in the Water Act of 2002. A summary of the main features of each of these instruments of change and some of their major proposals is given below. Previous attempts at reform are also described to give an overview of the history, achievements and challenges.

National Water and Sanitation Policy, 1999

The policy has four broad objectives:

(a)   To preserve, conserve and protect available water resources and allocate them in a sustainable, rational and economic way.

(b)   To supply water of good quality and in sufficient quantities to meet the various water needs while ensuring safe disposal of wastewater and environmental protection.

(c)   To establish an efficient and effective Institutional Framework to achieve systematic development and management of the water sector, and promote and support comprehensive participation of water users.

(d)   To develop a sound and sustainable financing mechanism for effective water resources management and water supply and sanitation development.

To meet these four objectives, the policy statements can be summarized in the following sub-sections:

Water resources management

(a)   All efforts will be made to conserve water and its use will be regulated so as to benefit as many people and sectors as possible.

(b)   Water levies and fees will be introduced where necessary and applied to the use of water from all public water courses.

(c)   Decision-making with respect to water resource management will be decentralized by adopting four water resource management levels (national, basin, sub-basin, and catchment levels).

A national standing committee will deal with cross-sectoral issues.

Water and sewerage development

(a)   The government will continue to play a major role in the development of the water sector.

(b)   The government will remain committed to creating an enabling environment to help all actors to operate effectively and efficiently.

(c)   The government will adopt a diminishing role in the direct implementation of water supply and sanitation projects.

(d)   The government will fully encourage the active participation of beneficiaries in the development and operation of water supplies.

Institutional framework

(a)   The role of the government will be redefined with a new emphasis on regulatory and enabling functions as opposed to direct provision.

(b)   The government will support private sector participation and community management of services.

(c)   The ministry in charge of water will clearly define the roles of all actors and establish mechanisms to monitor the performance indicators for all actors.

(d)   The government will endeavour to hand over rural water supplies to the communities.

Financing of water sector

(a)   Water should be considered as an economic good, and all water consumers should pay for water on the basis of the 'user pays' principle.

(b)   Effluent discharge levies will be introduced.

(c)   Management of the financial resources of the water sector will continue to be as per the government's regulations.

Principles and justifications

The policy redefines the roles of the various actors, and this is accompanied by institutional reforms that promote an integrated approach to water management. Key to these changes are the following principles:

(a)   Separation of policy, regulatory and implementation functions within the water and sewerage sector and, in the process, the streamlining of the roles of the various actors.

(b)   Separation of water resource management from provision of water and sewerage services. This avoids conflicts of interest in resource allocation and management. The government does what it does best throughout the world – enforcement and oversight – while other players efficiently provide the actual service using tested commercial principles in service provision within a performance-based incentive framework.

(c)   Devolution of responsibilities to local authorities, communities and other actors to create a sense of ownership and responsibility.

(d)   Provision of autonomy to service providers to enhance performance without political interference.

Previous and current attempts

Over the years, massive changes in the mode of operation, management and development of infrastructure have taken place. The population has increased from 6 million at independence in 1963 to over 33 million in 2004. The patterns of land use have also changed, with 86 per cent of the land being semi-arid and 5 per cent reserved for National Parks. More than 80 per cent of the population is carried by only 4 per cent of the land area.

Of the 33 million people, 65 per cent are rural and 35 per cent urban. Of the urban population, more than 60 per cent is estimated to live in unplanned informal settlements with rudimentary infrastructure for service provision. In the year 2000, there were an estimated 742,000 water connections serving a population of about 14 million. Out of this, the urban population of 8.2 million is served by 430,000 connections while the rest of the connections serve the rural population (World Bank, 2000).

The Water Act 2002 that replaced the previous Water Act (which was known as 'Cap 372') provides the enabling legal and institutional framework for more effective management, conservation, use and control of water resources and for the acquisition and regulation of rights to use water. It also provides for the regulation and management of water supply and sewerage services. A key complementary policy to the Water Act is the Economic Recovery Strategy Paper for Wealth and Employment Creation for 2003–07 (GoK, 2003b).

The strategy paper encourages more active involvement of the private sector in the development and management of water resources. The policy implementation process started with the enactment of the Water Act 2002 in March 2003. The implementation process is already underway, with the constitution of the principal institutions mandated to drive the process forward. Among these are the Water Resources Management Authority (WRMA), constituted in December 2003, and the Water Services Regulatory Board (WSRB).

The WSRB has been overseeing the establishment and operationalization of decentralized and autonomous Water Services Boards (WSBs) that will in turn appoint the Water Service Providers (WSPs). In some urban areas, WSPs had been established on a pilot basis under the sessional paper work. The performance of these WSPs has been mixed, with the utilities from Nyeri and Eldoret considered successful examples. The City of Nairobi established the Nairobi City Water and Sewerage Company Limited in early 2004.

Roles of the new institutions
In the institutional structure, the ministry in charge of water affairs will be responsible for policy formulation, sector coordination and financing. Other major roles include carrying out research, and the training and registration of professionals. The ministry will also establish the relevant institutions in support of the above actors, approve and coordinate budgets for WSBs, and liaise with donors to channel funds for he development of water services.

The WSRB, whose only link with the Ministry of Water Affairs is through legislation, regulates matters of water supply and sanitation service provision through the direct supervision of the WSBs. The Boards will provide services by entering into contracts with licensed WSPs appointed through competitive tendering. The WSBs will come into operation in areas delineated under Cap 372 and based on viability studies, and will sub-contract most of the tasks related to the selection of private WSPs, preparation of projects and financing application.

The legal responsibility for providing water services is vested in the WSBs, who will also hold existing assets. WSBs may, where necessary, lease assets as well as owning them, and may also access loans using the assets as collateral. The WSBs are charged with preparing business plans for the operation and maintenance, development, and extension of WSS services. The Boards have a mandate to ensure that services are provided within their areas of coverage without leaving any gaps.

Any complaints from WSBs, WSPs and consumers about the provision of services and regulation are lodged and heard by the Appeals Board. The law says that water provision cannot be cut off while the appeals mechanism takes place. The minister approves the Appeals Board and the president appoints the chairman of the Appeals Board, on the recommendation of the Chief Justice. The WSBs will provide technical support to communities, self-help groups (SHGs), and NGOs delegated from the WSRB.

The WSPs include private sector participants (PSP), NGOs, communities, SHGs, etc. The WSPs are licensed by the WSRB to qualify to submit bids to operate the water facilities. Local authorities, especially in urban centres, may also form companies to bid for operation of services.

Financing mechanisms

The water sector has experienced a sharp decline in financing for both development and operation and maintenance over the years. The current funding levels available to the sector are very low compared to the 1970s and 1980s. This declining trend has continued to the point where the scarcity of financial resources both for development and rehabilitation of the existing water supplies poses the biggest challenge to the government. This is against the proclaimed objective of increasing water coverage.

Funding for operation and maintenance (O&M)

In the case of rural water supplies, facilities have continued to deteriorate due to inadequate allocation of funds for maintenance. Rural water supply's reliance on the government for O&M funding has proved futile due to declining allocations, which are about 40 per cent of water revenues collected.

Funding of O&M for urban water supply is a different problem as management is less reliant on the government. Lack of autonomy in the management of water supply and sanitation services has resulted in the diversion of water revenues to unrelated financial expenditure by local authorities. Unsustainable cross-subsides have undermined the operations of other providers e.g. the National Water Conservation and Pipeline Corporation (NWCPC) and Ministry of Water and Irrigation.

Funding for expansion and new schemes development
For both rural and urban water supplies and sanitation services, funding from the government and development partners has declined due to various reasons, including:

(a) Percentage of budget allocated for recurrent expenditure has increased in proportion to development expenditure, which has sharply declined.

(b) Financial institutions have shied away from supporting the water and sanitation sub-sector as it is considered a high-risk investment.

(c) Private funding has not been forthcoming to the sector, as water has not been viewed as an attractive business investment.

(d) External financing has been tied to macroeconomic reforms, which have taken a long time to be realized.

4.2   SWEs in the context of private sector participation (PSP)

The Water Service Boards are charged with improving bulk water infrastructure using the revenue generated from selling bulk water to service providers such as the private companies being formed by the local authorities.

Informal settlements have largely been ignored in the provision of water supply services as they are considered to be illegal and temporary. They do, however, have great business potential for SWEs, because of the large number of people who buy water in small quantities.

In discussions on water privatization and private sector participation, public–private partnership providers are usually assumed to be large private utilities, omitting the small informal private providers. These informal providers are already playing a major role in water provision in informal settlements where a large proportion of the population lives (in Nairobi more than 60 per cent of the population).

In informal settlements water distribution is done in 20-litre containers carried on the head, or using pushcarts or bicycles. Tankers complement the public supply in the high-income areas. This way public and private systems often complement one another in providing and distributing water in the City of Nairobi.

Harper (2000) shows that effective public sector service delivery by small- and micro-enterprises (SMEs) is associated with public authorities taking on (or confining themselves to) the following key roles:

- Regulating and monitoring the activities of the enterprise

- Supplying facilities, goods and equipment

- Owning larger assets

- Providing part of the service

The most effective improvements in services arose where utilities were able to relinquish relevant aspects of their 'monopoly' control, but still establish an effective business relationship with private micro-entrepreneurs. The most frequent business relationship reported by Harper is the sub-contracting of all or part of the service delivery. Plummer and Gentry (2002) describe in detail various forms of organizational and contractual arrangements that arise in contracting formal enterprises, including service contracts, lease contracts, franchises and concessions.

They also point out that although SMEs can, in principle, be contracted through similar mechanisms, this usually requires the SMEs to register formally as legal entities. This is frequently a very difficult or inaccessible procedure. There appears to be very little literature describing experiences in establishing SME partnerships for water service delivery. The implication is that regularized partnerships between SMEs/SWEs and water utilities or authorities are still very rare.

4.3   Land tenure in informal settlements

This study found that land tenure in Maili Saba is quasi-legal, with residents holding no legal title to land but having the agreement of the local chiefs to build and settle in Maili Saba. Provisions have been made to allocate portions of land to the current occupants.

It is often argued that tenure issues must be solved before improving water services, as there is a fear that to do otherwise would give these settlements some semblance of legality. Considering that land tenure issues are unlikely to be resolved immediately, it might be prudent to look for alternative options for providing water infrastructure in the informal settlements, on the basis that informal settlements are here to stay, at least in the short and medium term. Informal settlements have been recognized as the home of the urban work force, and they are normally the backbone of production industries and also create a large consumer market.

Experience shows that it is now possible to provide sustainable water and sanitation services in informal settlements if it is done with the full participation and involvement of the beneficiary community. The guiding principle is to help the communities improve their water services by investing in affordable, appropriate and sustainable water service systems and technologies. Successful approaches are therefore user based and demand driven.

4.4   Millennium Development Goals

The Millennium Development Goal for water aims to reduce by half the number of people without access to safe water by the year 2015. The government of Kenya ratified the MDGs, but has had a slow start in implementing them. According to a ministerial statement, the country in now on track and starting in 2004 the ministry plans to make annual updates on the progress of the water MDG.

On the other hand, development expenditure in the water sector has been erratic over the years. It was KSh2,141,000 in 1992 and peaked at KSh43,098,000 in 1995 before declining to KSh34,554,000 in 1996/97. This trend has continued to the point where the scarcity of financial resource both for the development and rehabilitation of the existing water supplies poses the biggest challenge to the government (GoK, 1999:5).

4.5   Incentives to serve the poor

In the context of poverty reduction, both donors and the government are putting more emphasis on providing basic services to the poor. The 2002 Poverty Reduction Strategy Paper (PRSP) recognizes the provision of water and sanitation as a key element to alleviating abject poverty. In this light, concerns regarding services to the poor by SWEs could be addressed through the:

- skilful design of private sector contracts/concessions;

- creation of partnerships between SWEs and local/national government;

- policy of making service to the poor a part of the regulatory framework; and

- encouragement of technological innovation and non-conventional ways to deliver services to low-income areas, including the use of low-cost options and different levels of service to serve the poor.

In practice, a major element of supporting SWEs lies in creating an operating environment that protects them from harassment and extortion. Recognizing and regularizing their role at municipal authority level may at least help reduce rent-seeking by officials.

A need for 'capacity building' initiatives for SWEs is identified as a way of making SWEs organize themselves and voice their needs/concerns.

Other incentives relevant to SWEs may include:

- support for accessing micro-credit (e.g. group facilitation and information);
- leasing of transport equipment and vending facilities;
- rental of secure premises for storing equipment; and
- management (operation and maintenance) of water supply points.

4.6   Water, gender and poverty

During the last few years, there has been some interest in applying the sustainable livelihoods framework to the water sector (Moriarty, 2002; Nicol, 2000). The framework places considerable emphasis on assets and the contribution of assets to people's well-being and security. Assets are divided into financial, social, physical, natural and human. Water can be viewed both as an asset and as a factor influencing access to other assets. In particular, health is an important component of human capital. The relationship between water availability and the incidence of diseases has long been acknowledged (e.g. Hardoy et al, 2001; Thompson et al, 2000; and Stephens, 1996). It is recognized that low-income areas lack basic services and infrastructure and that this leads to significant health problems.

Etherington et al (2002) show that medical costs and lost wages from disease consume a large part of household income for the poor. Such problems reflect both the availability of water of sufficient quality and quantity and the way people dispose of wastewater. The importance of water, however, extends beyond the health issues. Thompson et al (2000) argue that a lack of access to adequate and affordable water has several important consequences for livelihoods, such as increased costs, time and physical effort to obtain water, reduced consumption, increased health burdens and lost productivity.

Thompson et al (2000) described the contribution of water to household livelihoods when they discussed three broad categories of water use: consumption, hygiene, and amenities. In a detailed study of nine East African towns and cities they identified the following priority uses: drinking, cooking, bathing, cleaning, washing, gardening and beer-brewing. Reflecting on these activities, it may be useful to augment their three-fold categories of water use to specifically include production-related activities in addition to consumption, hygiene and amenities. In such uses, water makes a critical contribution to poverty reduction.

4.7   Trends

With an annual population growth rate estimated at 7–10 per cent, Nairobi will continue to experience an influx of people from the rural areas, with most of the newcomers ending up in the informal settlements. This will overstress the already-stressed service infrastructure. Water demand in the informal settlements is expected to rise. The role of SWEs in meeting this demand among the poor is expected to become more important. However, the price of water will rise and the quality of service will deteriorate. From this perspective, an intervention that mainstreams SWEs into the urban water supply chain will have a positive impact on the consumer as well as on SWEs themselves.

Chapter 5

Informal Settlements in Nairobi

5.1 Introduction

This chapter describes the general situation of informal settlements in Nairobi, using the Maili Saba informal settlement as a case study. It is based on field findings and conclusions from the literature survey conducted for this research project.

All major informal settlements in Nairobi have developed along the valleys of the Nairobi River or its tributaries, or along the railway line. Consequently, human activity in slums has been a major factor contributing to the pollution of the Nairobi River system. Most informal settlements are in areas that were once excavated for quarrying and therefore do not attract high-class residential areas.

5.2 Maili Saba informal settlement – The case study

Maili Saba informal settlement is about 10 km east of Nairobi city centre. It has a population of 9,872 people (3,368 households) and covers an area of about 3.9 km², giving a population density of 2,531 people per square kilometre. The main water supply utility is Nairobi City Council's Water and Sanitation Department (now Nairobi Water and Sanitation Company Limited). The criteria used to select Maili Saba for this case study included:

- It has a high population density.
- It is not served by the main public/municipal utility.
- The settlement is illegal.
- The settlement has a low supply volume.
- The water is not inspected.
- There is poor access to water and intermittent supply.
- Water distribution is through direct vending, not tankers.
- Plots are not owned by Nairobi City Council nor by private developers.

Kibera, the biggest informal settlement in Nairobi, was not surveyed because the area is generally over studied and the residents are getting more sensitive to researchers who don't seem to change life for them. Under the characteristics described above, Maili Saba was ranked fourth out of 12 settlements. The first three, Githurai, Soweto, and Quarry, were discounted because they are influenced by areas beyond the borders of Nairobi. The choice of Maili Saba was further influenced by the fact that the research institution already had activities in the area and this made access easy. The scoring for each of the 12 settlements is shown in Table 5.1. and the key to scoring criteria in Table 5.2.

Table 5.1. Scores for each of 12 settlements considered for case study									
	Population Density	SWP	Legality	Utility	Inspections	Supply volumes	Accessibility	Ownership	Total
Githurai (Kamae/Soweto)	4	6	4	4	4	6	6	4	38
Soweto	6	4	4	2	4	6	6	2	34
Quarry	4	4	4	4	2	6	4	4	32
Maili Saba	4	4	4	2	4	4	4	4	30
Mukuru Kaiyaba	6	6	4	4	2	2	2	4	30
Sinai	4	6	4	4	2	2	2	4	28
Huruma	4	6	4	4	2	2	2	4	28
Kawangware	6	4	4	2	2	4	2	2	26
Kuwinda	2	2	4	2	2	6	6	2	26
Kangemi	4	4	4	2	2	4	4	2	26

Table 5.2. Key to scoring criteria				
Population density			**Utility**	
Low	2		Utility and borehole	2
Medium	4		Utility	4
High	6		Borehole	6
			Other	8
Legality			**Supply volume**	
Legal	2		Good	2
Legal and illegal	4		Medium	4
Illegal	6		Bad	6
Inspections by city council			**Accessibility to the village**	
Inspected	2		Good	2
Not inspected and inspected	4		Fair	4
Non inspected	6		Bad	6
Small water enterprises			**Ownership of the water supply**	
Wholesale, distributing and direct vending	2		Utility and Private	2
			Utility	4
Distributing and direct	4		Other	6
Direct	6			

5.3 Water supply and other living conditions

All informal settlements are characterized by a lack of adequate physical planning, residents' low socio-economic status, a poverty-stricken population, overcrowding, inadequacy of water supply, lack of privacy (shared bathrooms, toilets, etc.), poor access by vehicles and pedestrians, and poor sanitary and environmental health conditions. The population census of 1999 revealed that some settlements have a population density of more than 82,000 people per square kilometre. Over the last two decades, HIV/AIDS has emerged as an added threat and challenge to the dwellers of the informal urban settlements.

> 'Some 100,000 people are leaving rural poverty every year to come to Nairobi. The economy is not able to give them employment, so they become a problem of the city. Nairobi is taking the burden of the entire national economy.'
>
> Patrick Odongo, City Planning Department

In a working document entitled 'A Rapid Economic Appraisal of Rents in Slums and Informal Settlements', UN-HABITAT (2002) reports that 'apart from limited access to water sources, residents of informal settlements are not provided with basic services and infrastructure by urban authorities. Government authorities are unwilling or in some cases unable to provide basic water and sanitation services to the majority of residents in informal settlements.'

Housing

The research observed that 71 per cent of people in the informal settlements under study live in structures that they own, and 29 per cent live in rented accommodation. Most of these structures (41 per cent) have two rooms; the rest vary, with the highest number of rooms recorded being eight. Although structures may have several rooms, most families occupy a single room within a building. The survey shows that structures in Maili Saba are mainly made of mud (56 per cent) or corrugated iron sheeting (34 per cent) with an unmade earth floor. The rest have stone walls. Floors are mainly made of earth sprinkled with murram (67 per cent), although 33 per cent of households have cement floors. All the houses visited used iron sheets for the roof. About 90 percent of slum homes are single rooms measuring between 9 and 14 m² in area. Most rooms are occupied by about three people, although a few rooms accommodate up to five people.

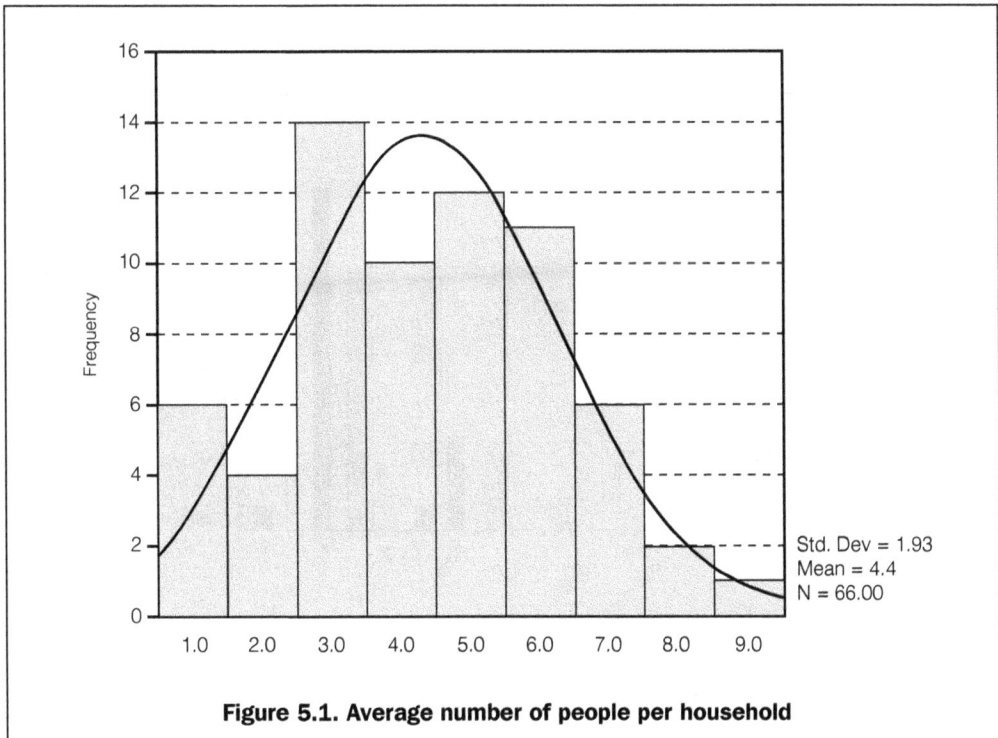

Figure 5.1. Average number of people per household

Household characteristics

The survey reveals an average of 4.4 people per household. The survey data provides a slightly larger household size than the figure of three people per household for Maili Saba. Some individuals live alone while highest recorded number of people in a house is nine. Figure 5.1 shows the distribution of individuals in households. The number of people per house is very variable.

Occupation

Most residents are employed either in the informal sector or in low-paying jobs in the industrial area of the city. The informal sector predominates, including petty businesses, open-air garages, the hawking of various wares, and the informal manufacturing of small articles by artisans known as juakali (Swahili for 'hot sun', because most work is in the open air). In the informal settlements commerce means any woman selling vegetables and any man selling second-hand clothes.

Employment opportunities have included working as day-labourers in the nearby industrial area and as drivers, shop stewards, and sweepers. Some work as juakali artisans, house-helps, or labourers in the stone and murram quarries. Those with additional rooms rent them out to earn income. The makers and sellers of illicit brews are plentiful, as are commercial sex workers, due to the lack of alternative employment opportunities.

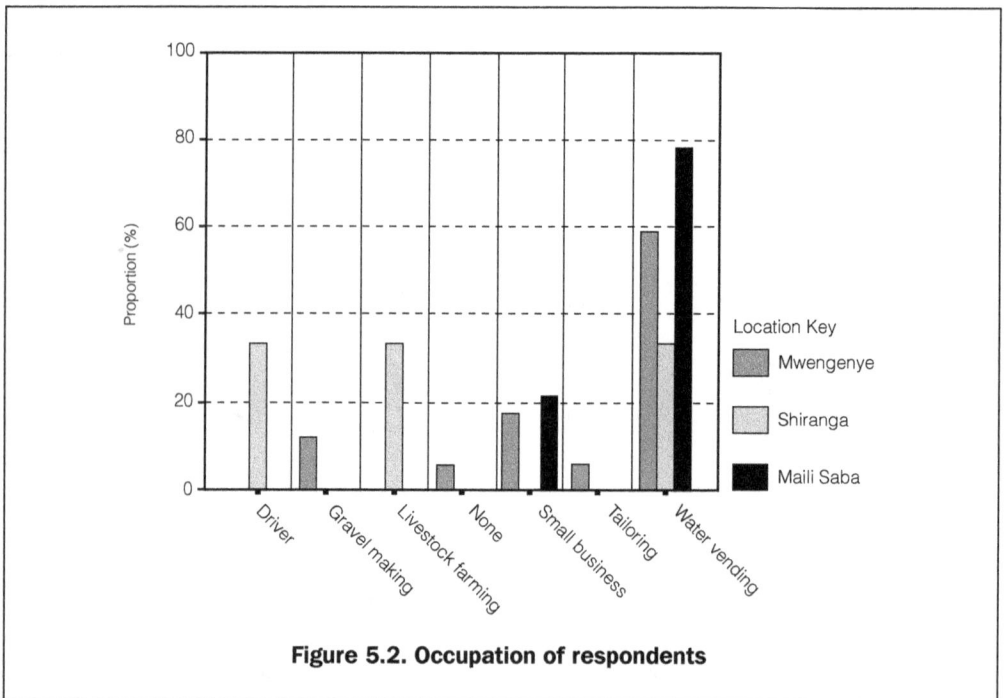

Figure 5.2. Occupation of respondents

Figures 5.2 and 5.3 show the occupation of respondents in Mwengenye, Shiranga and Maili Saba, and information about family members in employment elsewhere. It should be noted that the respondents are not representative of the areas where they live, and a high number of respondents were engaged in water vending.

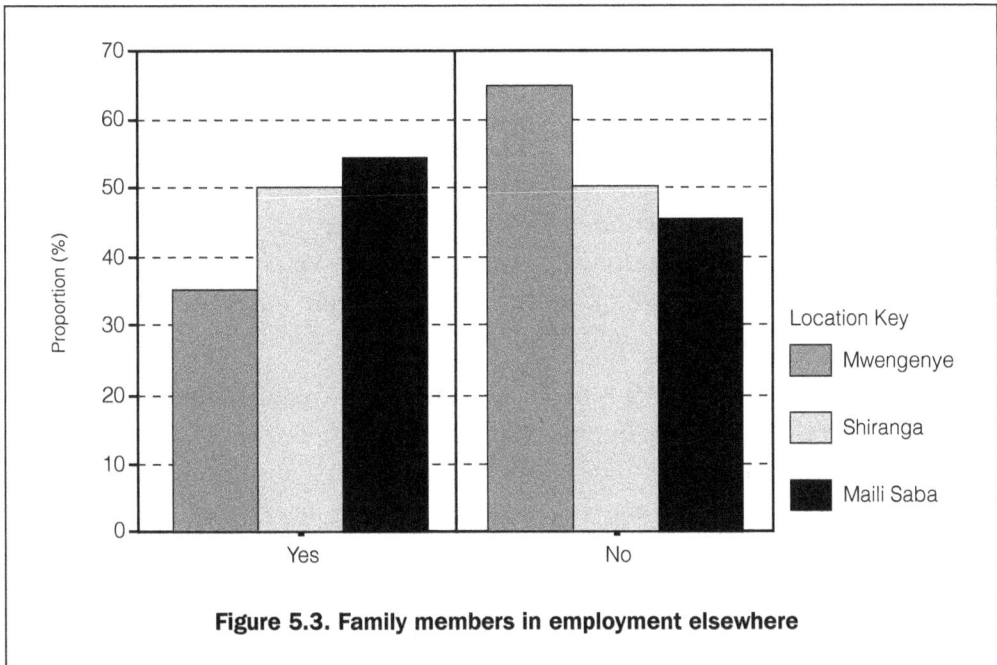

Figure 5.3. Family members in employment elsewhere

Box 5.1. Informal settlements in Nairobi: Fact Sheet

- Occupy about 10% of the city's land area
- Home to about 60% (1.8 million) of the population
- Growth rate of 7 to 12% per year
- Classified as temporary
- Some have existed for nearly 100 years
- Classified as illegal or quasi-legal
- Provision of services to the informal settlements is poor or non-existent
- Majority of residents live below the poverty level

Land ownership

Much of the land on which the slums have been constructed is publicly owned. This means that landlords are not legally obliged to provide any services – which results in no latrines, water, electricity, or solid waste collection. Infrastructure is poor or non-existent and housing is poor, with open sewers and unhealthy living conditions.

Maili Saba is located on government-owned land. The residents report that they were allowed to settle temporarily by the Nairobi Provincial Administration. It is reported that the land was sub-divided to the temporary owners in 1996.

The land tenure of the settlement is described as quasi–legal as the residents hold no legal ownership to the land although they have been given the mandate to settle there by the local administration. Legal provisions have been made to allocate portions of land to the current occupiers. although some allocations have fallen into undeserving hands as a result of spontaneous evictions.

Urban agriculture is practised, where the community members block sewers to obtain water for irrigation. Some keep some livestock.

5.4　The policy and slum upgrading programme

There is no national policy on slum upgrading, no regularization of land allocation procedures, no guaranteed security of tenure for slum dwellers, no laws to prevent the construction of slum houses lacking basic amenities such as access to water and latrines, and no recognition by government of the citizenship and corresponding rights of Nairobi's slum dwellers. In 2002 UN-Habitat signed a memorandum of understanding under which the UN body would support the government to formulate policy guidelines and seek funding for a slum-upgrading project.

The Kenya Slum Upgrading Project is a major initiative by the Kenyan government's Department of Housing aimed at improving living conditions for slum dwellers in Nairobi. The objectives include ensuring security of tenure and improving physical infrastructure (roads, water, sanitation, health, and schools) and other social services. In line with other best practices from around the world, tenants and landlords will be consulted and fully involved in the planning and execution phases of the slum upgrading project to ensure that their needs and concerns are addressed.

The upgrading project would entail the temporary relocation of slum dwellers to enable contractors to build better homes for them. But many are jittery over the project, including the owners of shacks rented out to slum dwellers, rent collectors, tenants afraid of losing their homes, and charities and religious groups that collect money for the poor.

Chapter 6

Water Services and Poverty

6.1 Methodology

The methodology of assessing water services and poverty included a literature review, field surveys, and analysis. The literature review included published and grey literature and was carried out in order to:

- understand the urban water sector – management, supply, land use, livelihood linkages and delivery;

- analyse the role of various actors in the sector in Kenya – especially the government, utility, local authority, NGOs, and academia;

- review the emergence and development of water vending practices in Kenya; and

- analyse policy impacts on urban small-scale water provision with the aim of providing a comparative scenario on the current debate on urban water management.

The field survey included site selection, development and pre-testing of a checklist/questionnaire, and a field survey (focus group discussion, key informant interviews, observations and household interviews). Survey teams (seven research assistants of whom four were from the target village) undertook a field survey. The survey teams were trained in participatory survey methodologies for the survey and data collection. A checklist/questionnaire was developed, pre-tested and amended appropriately before being used in the survey. The field survey was conducted in Maili Saba from 19 to 24 January, 2004. A total of 34 SWEs and 66 consumers were randomly selected for interviewing. Table 6.1 shows the distribution of respondents by location.

Table 6.1. Distribution of respondents by location

Respondents		Location			
		Mwengenye	Shilanga	Maili Saba	Total
Household	Female	26	14	8	48
	Male	6	1	2	9
	Total	32	15	10	57
Construction	Male			2	2
	Total			2	2
Hotel	Female		2	1	3
	Male	1	1	2	4
	Total	1	3	3	7

Structured and semi-structured interview schedules (questionnaires) were used to collect the information needed for the study. Focus group discussions were also conducted to further clarify and prioritize water issues in the study areas. The survey team used observation and checklists to gather visual information that could not be collected through interviews. The mapping of key water points was also done to profile the spatial distribution of water points. Information was collected, sifted, coded and entered into a statistical package for social sciences (SPSS), where it was analysed. The study also made use of anecdotal evidence from respondents. Workshops were conducted to triangulate and validate the information collected from the various field surveys and segments.

Data from unpublished ITDG surveys in 2001 and 2004 indicates that in 2001 approximately 48% of households had monthly incomes below KSh5,000; but by 2004 approximately 90% of households had monthly incomes below KSh5,000. It is apparent from figures that incomes have largely deteriorated, but this could be for a variety of reasons, including the survey methodology, as the two studies did not use the same sampling frame.

6.2   Water resources use in Nairobi

According to a survey conducted by the company Seureca in 1998, the current overall daily water production in Nairobi closely meets the estimated daily water requirements of 320,000 m³ . However, the distribution is erratic and there are huge losses due to leakages. Between 93 and 97 per cent of the water consumed in Nairobi comes from the utility's water supply. Only a few consumers, almost exclusively in the Karen and Lang'ata areas, have private boreholes.

The majority of residents in informal settlements do not have direct connections to the utility's pipeline. They mainly purchase water from waterpoints (standpipes, water kiosks and vendors). The tariffs for water are structured in blocks depending on usage. Bulk water purchasers, including water kiosks, buy water at US$0.15 per 1000 litres. Water at the standpipes (kiosks) sells at US$1.25/m³ during normal supply and this rises to US$3/m³ during short supply. When the same amount of water is delivered to the households it costs US$10/m³ for domestic consumers and US$15/m³ for commercial and construction sites. Thus the low-income earners living in informal settlements spend as much as ten times more than the consumers directly connected to the Nairobi City Council water supply (Njoroge and Obel-Lawson, 2000).

6.3   Household income and water expenditure

The average distance to a waterpoint in Kibera is 40 m (Njoroge and Obel-Lowson, 2000) and in Maili Saba it is estimated to be 250 m (ITDG, 2004).

The main sources of income (61 per cent of the respondents) in Maili Saba are small businesses (9 per cent) and informal employment (52 per cent). This includes selling vegetables, running small kiosks, or crushing and selling gravel to local builders. Those engaged in informal employment work , such as working as home helps, watchmen, waiters and cooks in small restaurants make up 52 per cent of respondents. A few individuals own rental houses (6 per cent), have formal employment (5 per cent), and some are privileged to receive remittances (2 per cent) from friends, family members and relatives. Some of the respondents had more than one source of income. Note that the information shown in Figure 5.2 refers to respondents, of whom a high percentage were engaged in water vending.

On average, the monthly household income of respondents is KSh6,406 (equivalent to US$84), meaning they live on an average of 2.8 dollars a day per household. However, the poorest households earn as low as KSh700 (US$9) per month and the richest earn over KSh25,000 (US$329) per month. Figure 6.1 indicates that 15 per cent of respondents in Maili Saba earn less than a dollar a day, 54 per cent earn up to US$3, and approximately 31 per cent earn more than US$3 per day.

Average monthly income

The average monthly expenditure is KSh5,327 (US$70). The greatest expenditure is on food (67 per cent), water (9 per cent), education (13 per cent), and 18 per cent is spent on miscellaneous items. This survey therefore revealed that some people spend as much money as they earn, commonly referred to as 'hand to mouth' living.

A household with an average of six people spends US$6.30 a month on water, or about US$1 per person per month. If these households were connected to the utility mains they would receive 40 m³ of water per month delivered to their house for the same amount of money they spend now. This could deliver to poor households an average of 200 litres per person per day, well within recommended per person per day water consumption. Currently with their spend of US$6.30 per month they can collect from the kiosks barely 5 m³ during normal supply and 2 m³ per month during shortages. The average daily water consumption per person is 27 litres during normal supply and barely 12 litres per person during the periods of short supply.

The potential exists for the utility to harness the markets in the informal settlements with an estimated 1.8 million people willing to pay and currently spending an average of US$1 per month for a very low level of service. The main challenges are the investment costs, willingness on the part of the utility to improve services to users in informal settlements, and general public apathy to pay for what is seen as a public service that ought to be provided free of charge for users.

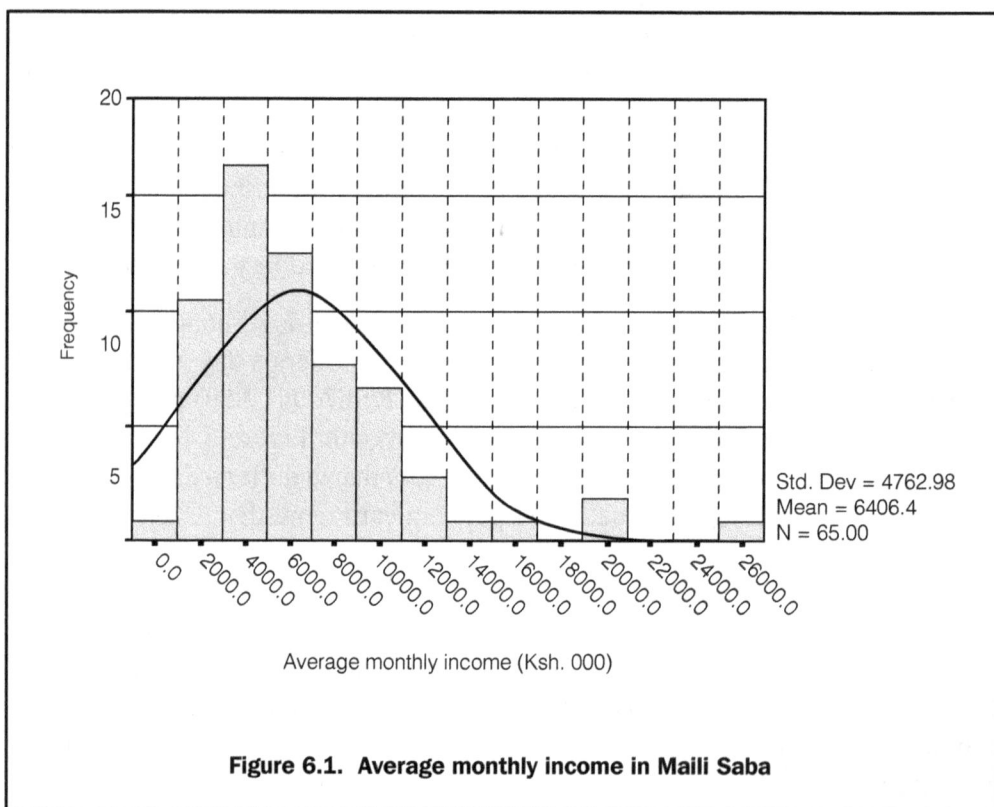

Std. Dev = 4762.98
Mean = 6406.4
N = 65.00

Average monthly income (Ksh. 000)

Figure 6.1. Average monthly income in Maili Saba

6.4   Patterns of water usage

This section analyses the various sources and uses of water for residents in informal settlements, the amount of water consumed, distance covered, and time spent to collect water. Other aspects such as cost, quality and reliability have also been covered in this section.

The survey explored the main sources of water in Maili Saba as identified by the consumers/water users, including:
• water supply through direct connection to Nairobi City Council mains;

• water purchased by collection from kiosks;

• water purchased from bicycle and backload vendors; and

• boreholes, wells, springs and rainwater catchments.

The findings showed that kiosks are the main source of water, supplying about 70 per cent of the residents directly. All the kiosk operators get their water from the utility. Figure 6.2 below shows the distribution of water sourcing.

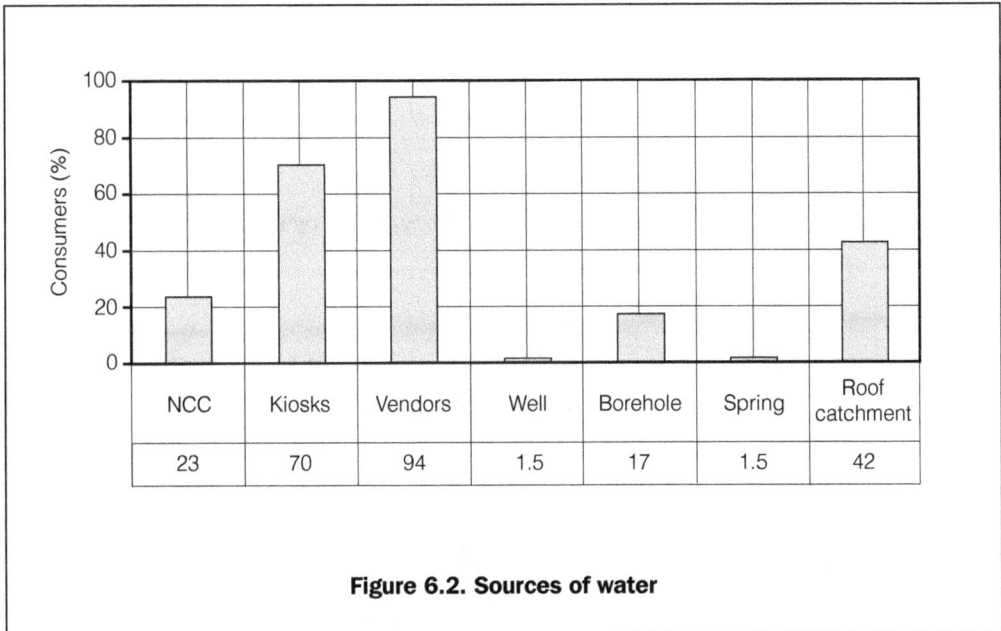

	NCC	Kiosks	Vendors	Well	Borehole	Spring	Roof catchment
	23	70	94	1.5	17	1.5	42

Figure 6.2. Sources of water

Nairobi City Council water supply is the single most important source of water in Maili Saba. This is supplemented by individual boreholes and some shallow wells within the locality. A river that flows through the settlement is also used, while rainwater is not adequately developed. The supply chain makes the utility the primary source, to which water kiosks are connected from which other vendors buy water for sale to their clients.

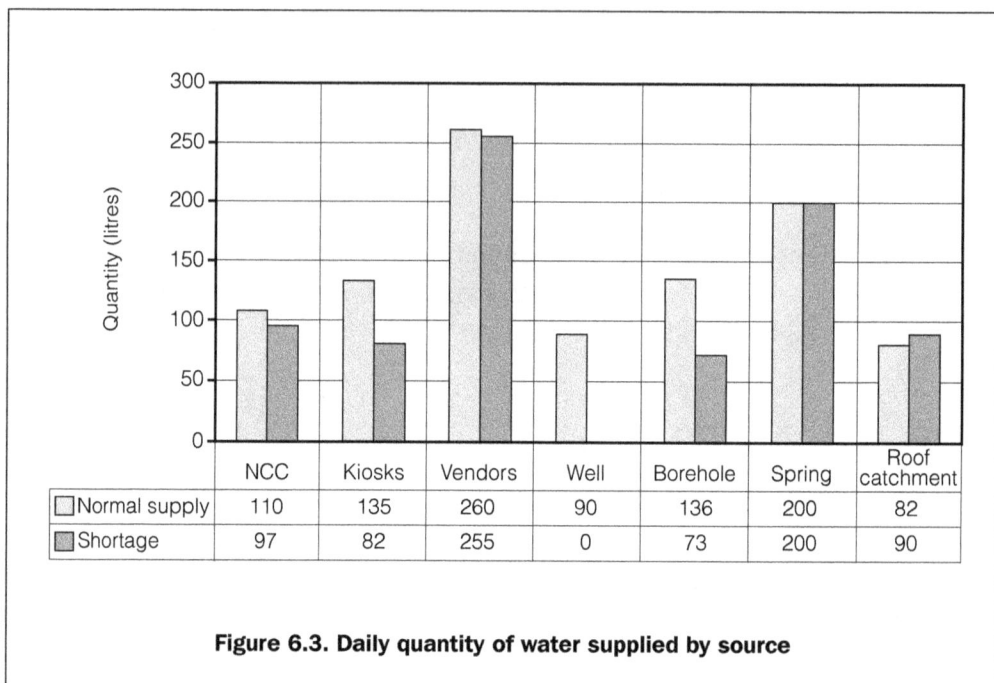

	NCC	Kiosks	Vendors	Well	Borehole	Spring	Roof catchment
Normal supply	110	135	260	90	136	200	82
Shortage	97	82	255	0	73	200	90

Figure 6.3. Daily quantity of water supplied by source

Water consumption is also influenced by the season and by normal and shortage periods. During normal supply, a 20-litre jerrycan of water from the kiosks costs approximately KSh3, but doubles to KSh6 when water is scare. Water vendors charge approximately KSh8 when the supply is good, which rises to almost KSh12 during shortages. The church-based borehole's costs remains relatively constant at KSh2 during both normal and short supply.

The most important water end-uses were drinking water (97 per cent of respondents), cooking (91 per cent) and washing utensils (68 per cent). Washing clothes, and bathing and house cleaning (40 per cent and 52 per cent respectively) came next. Table 6.3 shows rankings of relative importance of water needs by gender.

Table 6.2. Relative importance of water needs by gender

Location of respondent	Gender of respondent	Drinking			Cooking			Utensils (washing)			Clothes (washing)		
		A	B	C	A	B	C	A	B	C	A	B	C
Mwengenye	Female	26			24	2		19	7		3	7	15
	Male	7			5	2		5	7	2	3	7	7
	All	33			29	4		24	7	2			22
Shilanga	Female	16			15	1		13	3		1	6	9
	Male	2			2			1	1		1	1	1
	All	18			17	1		14	4		1	7	10
Maili Saba	Female	8			8	1		2	7		1	7	2
	Male	4	1	1	5			4	1		1	4	2
	All	12	1	1	13	1		6	8		1	11	2

Ranking: A = Very important B = Important C = Least important

It was further noted that water end-use also depended on source, for instance water from the utility, kiosks and vendors is mainly used for construction, cooking, drinking, washing utensils/clothes and brewing alcohol. Well water is mainly used to clean houses and latrines, for bathing and washing, and sometimes for cooking. Other residents use it for sprinkling on the earth floor to keep dust down. Borehole water is used for brewing alcohol, cooking, washing, bathing and drinking. Spring water is used for washing, cooking and sometimes drinking. Water from roof catchments is used for cooking, bathing, washing, and drinking.

Table 6.3 shows average daily quantity of water consumed by various uses.

Table 6.3. Average daily water consumption for various uses (litres)						
Respondent	Drinking	Cooking	Washing utensils	Washing clothes	Bathing and house cleaning	Other uses
Household	9.6	18	16	46	28	43
Construction	20	20	20	20	40	150
Hotel	34	116	40	30	24	-
Weighted average	12	29	18	44	29	64

Gender roles in water supply

Responsibility for water collection and even payment is bestowed upon the women. They also make decisions about where and whom to buy from, and how much water should be bought. People who live alone make their water purchasing decisions themselves. Table 6.4 is a summary of the gender roles of household members in water purchase. Different individuals may buy water at different times, and from different suppliers. The percentages shown in Table 6.4 do not therefore total to 100%.

The eldest female in the house decides on quality and how water will be used in the household. Clearly women are the main stakeholders in water matters in the informal settlements. Any improvements will directly improve their well-being and give them opportunities to improve their livelihoods by engaging in productive economic ventures.

Table 6.4. Responsibilites for water collection percentages			
	Who buys water (%)	Whom to buy from (%)	How much water to buy (%)
Women	67	73	73
Men	6	6	6
Children	18	3	3
House-help	3	-	-
Self	11	11	11
Family	-	2	-
No choice	2	-	-

Water accessibility to consumers in Maili Saba

Approximately 16 per cent of individuals interviewed have water delivered to their homes while the rest (84 per cent) fetch it. However, 53 per cent of respondents who prefer to fetch do it in the morning, while 20 per cent fetch water in both the morning and evenings, while 9 per cent fetch it any time.

Much more time is spent collecting water during shortages than during normal supply. The results from the analysis show that residents spent an average of 17 minutes to collect water during normal supply. During shortages, however, an average of 2 hours is spent collecting water. The least amount of time recorded is less than an hour to 8 hours. Figure 6.4 shows time used to collect water during normal and short supply.

It was worth noting that 16 per cent of respondents are willing to pay to have water delivered to their residences, despite the low income levels and high premium on the cost of delivery. Having water delivered to the household costs an equivalent of US$10/m^3 while a similar amount would cost an equivalent of US$1.25/m^3 during normal supply. From this observation it may be concluded that the residents in these poor informal settlements are willing to receive and pay for a higher level of service. It also speaks to the fact that despite the short average time of 17 minutes spent to collect water the time of these households is at premium in seeking alternative employment/commercial opportunities to make a living.

Reliability of supply is of greater value to the users at the current cost levels.

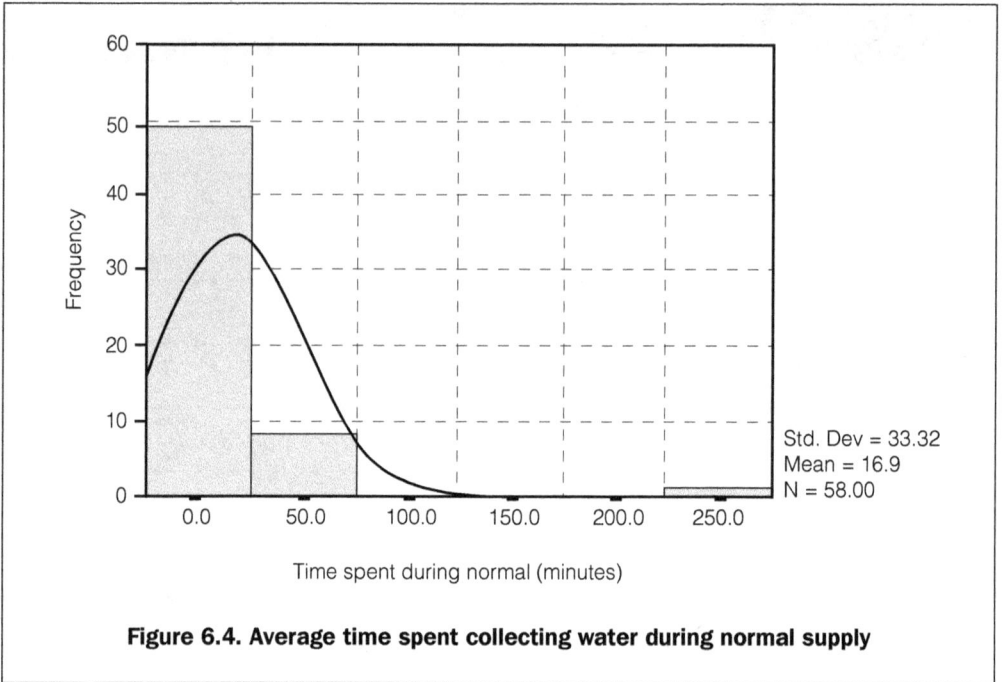

Figure 6.4. Average time spent collecting water during normal supply

Std. Dev = 33.32
Mean = 16.9
N = 58.00

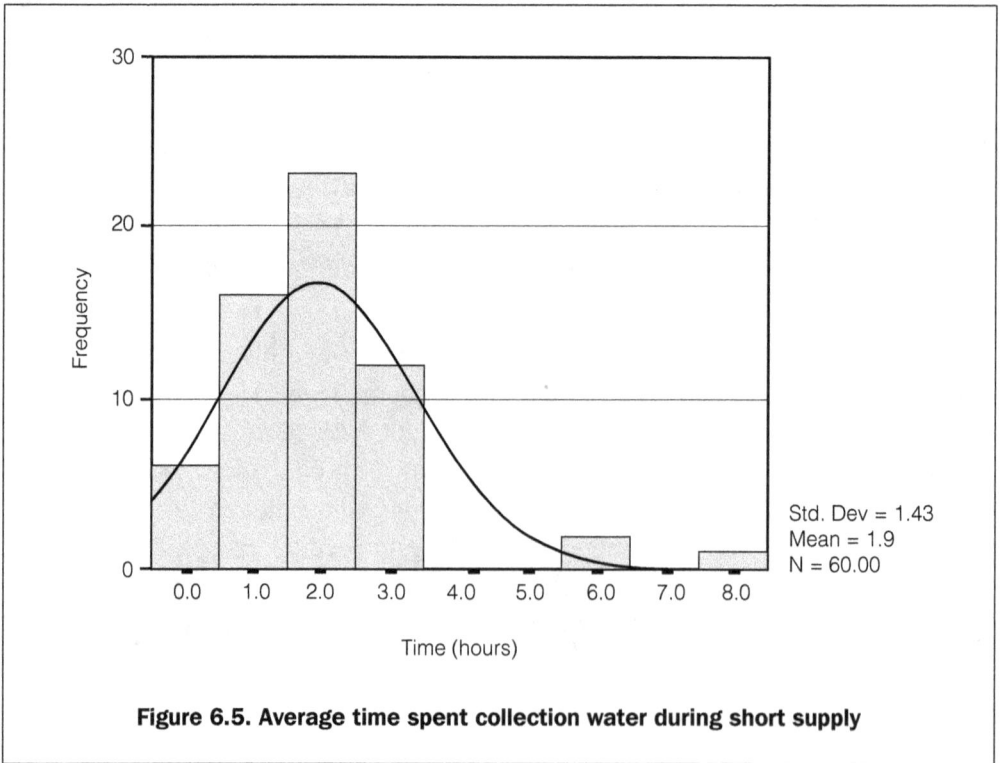

Figure 6.5. Average time spent collection water during short supply

Std. Dev = 1.43
Mean = 1.9
N = 60.00

6.5 Coping mechanisms

Poorer households develop coping mechanisms to ensure household water supplies. These include collecting water directly from the kiosk instead of buying it from vendors, collecting water from unprotected sources for some chores (washing), and reducing the amount of water used. These households are extremely vulnerable during shortages.

Other households boil their drinking water as a means of improving quality, which leads to increased fuel costs (usually charcoal).

The use of multiple sources exposes consumers to increased health risks.

Despite chronic water shortages, consumers have not made notable efforts to improve their water storage facilities, because of financial constraints.

6.6 Consumer perceptions of health and water quality

Poor water quality is a health risk. Most of the respondents cited the prevalence of water-related illnesses, such as typhoid, diarrhoea and stomach aches. Dental problems as a result of poor water quality were also reported. Some 59 per cent of people boil water before using it.

The disposal of sewage and wastewater is poor, resulting in pools of stagnant water and increased mosquito and rodent breeding. Malaria is a common ailment in the area.

Sewage and wastewater disposal methods include trenches, roads, pit latrines, garbage heaps and a few people irrigate their vegetable gardens.

Water storage capacity and the cost of water storage within the settlement is quite low, with households having a mean storage capacity of 344 litres that has cost them approximately KSh871. The smallest container is 20 litres, the largest 10,000 litres.

Chapter 7

Small Water Enterprises (SWEs)

7.1 Methodology

The selection of interviewees was done by random sampling. The survey village of Maili Saba was divided into three segments, and in each segment the survey team located themselves on the major pathways where the majority of the vendors operate.

The bicycle vendors and backloaders were interviewed while on duty. A kiosk vendor was asked to allow time to participate in the survey. Those who were willing to participate were interviewed or an appointment was made to interview them at their convenience. The kiosk owners were interviewed at their kiosks.

All the vendors were interviewed using pre-tested checklists and the responses were recorded in prepared formats.

Other participatory tools, including observations and focus group discussions, were also used.

7.2 SWEs overview

The residents of Maili Saba in Nairobi obtain their water mainly through SWEs. A typical household can choose from one the following services:

Directly from water kiosks: In this case a household member (usually women and children) collects water directly from the water kiosks. The labour is provided by the household and water is bought at KSh2 per 20 litres during normal supply. This may increase to KSh6 per 20 litres during short supply. Water collected in this way is of known quality. Some 70 per cent of the water used in households in Maili Saba is collected by the household directly.

Backloaders and bicycles vendors: These vendors buy water from the water kiosks and then resell it to the households or other clients (construction or hotels). They pay the kiosk price of KSh2 for 20 litres but resell the same quantity to clients for KSh10 or more.

Water kiosks: All kiosks get their water from the Nairobi City Council water system. Kiosks are makeshift structures or can be part of a home, with the water being sold through a window. In some cases the 'kiosk' is simply a standpipe.

Borehole: There is one borehole in the area. It is owned by a religious organization and supplies less that 2 per cent of the water used in Maili Saba during normal supply. It is a significant source during short supply.

Rivers, streams and wells: The water from these sources is heavily polluted and few people use it except for washing clothing. Very poor households use this source much more often than the wealthier households.

Rainwater harvesting: This option is not adequately developed in Maili Saba.

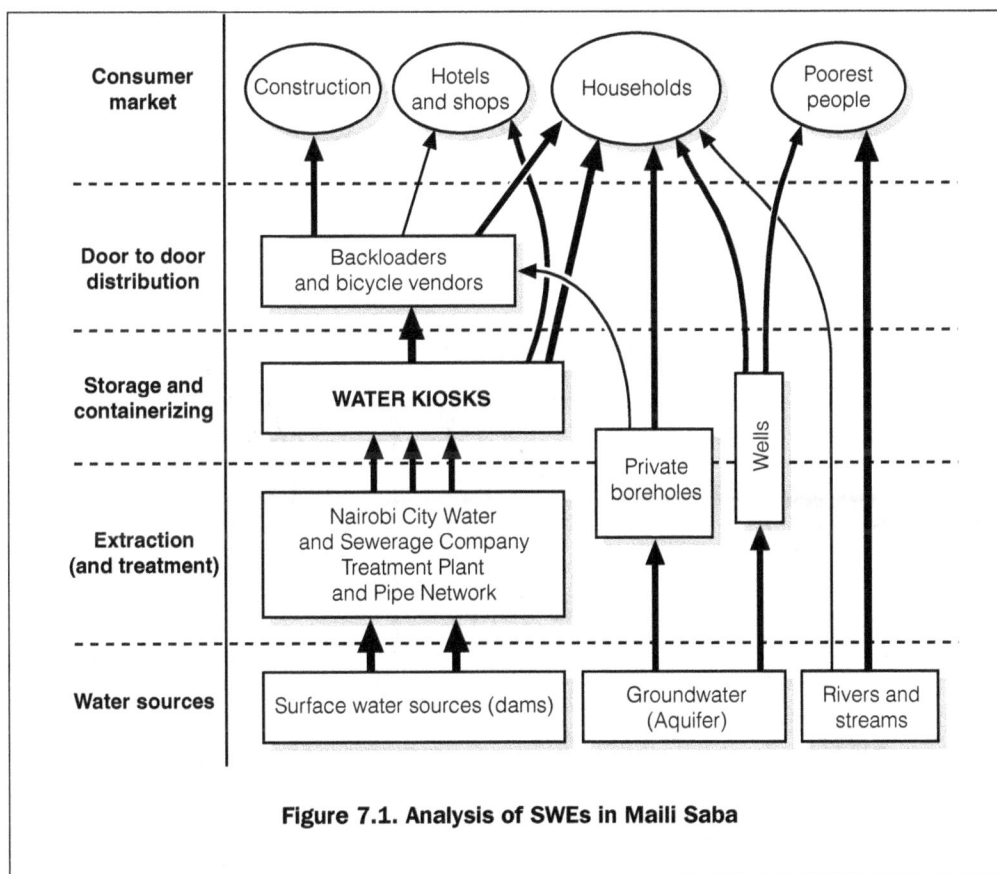

Figure 7.1. Analysis of SWEs in Maili Saba

7.3 Value chain analysis

The primary source of water is Nairobi City Council's water supply, where the basic rate is KSh12/m³ throughout the year.

This is the most important water source, supplying over 90 per cent of the water in the project area. The supplementary water sources include the individual boreholes, where water is sold for KSh100/m³ throughout the year. Water from the rivers, streams and wells is free but of doubtful quality.

The secondary level of the water chain includes the water kiosks, who buy all their water from the NWSC for KSh12/m³ and resell it to consumers (vendors and households) at KSh100–150/m³ during normal supply. This cost increases to over KSh300/m³ during shortages. In order to continue to supply their clients during the shortages, kiosk owners have invested in limited storage facilities. Most of the kiosks have metered connections and are charged KSh12/m³ for all the water they consume.

The third level of the water chain includes the bicycle vendors and backloaders. These vendors purchase water from kiosks and resell directly to households, construction sites, and restaurants and hotels. The minimum selling price is KSh5 per 20 litres (KSh250/m³) for domestic users, KSh16 per 20 litres for businesses, and KSh23 per 20 litres for construction. These prices vary significantly.

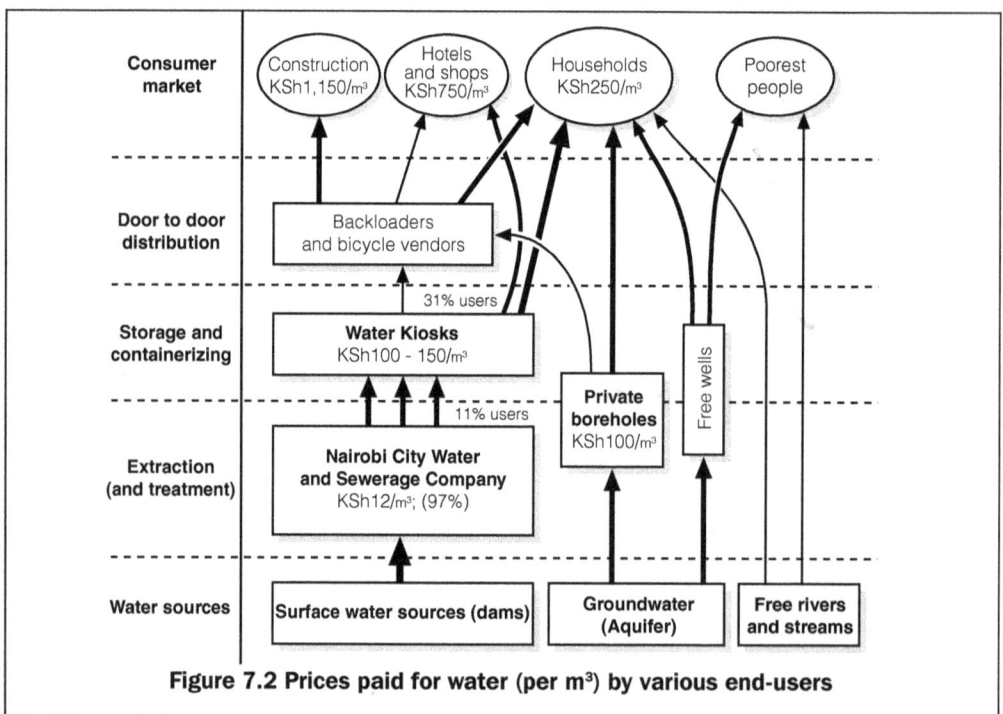

Figure 7.2 Prices paid for water (per m³) by various end-users

7.4   Livelihoods of SWE operators

All the 34 SWEs interviewed were Kenyans from various parts of the country. Most of the SWEs operate in the same area in which they live. Most (80 per cent) have lived in Maili Saba continuously during the last five years.

The majority of the SWEs are young people (50 per cent under 30) and only 10 per cent were over 50. The male:female mix is about 50:50, but the women are usually backloaders while the men use bicycles as well. About one in every four SWEs has a secondary-level education. Only a small minority (8 per cent) were illiterate.

Most SWEs have operated their business for more than three years, and 69 per cent of those interviewed said that vending is their full-time job, while 31 per cent have other part-time jobs. The longest serving SWE has been in the business for more than 22 years, making it a lifetime employment.

All the kiosk operators run their business on a full-time basis, and some have engaged other personnel to help run the business.

Start-up capital needed varies by the type of vending business. Kiosk operators have to apply for a licence from City Council, and upon receipt of the licence have to meet the installation costs. The total cost of setting up a water kiosk varies between KSh11,000 and KSh70,000, depending on the length of pipeline to be installed. The procedures were reported to be cumbersome and often required bribes. The procedures are not displayed on public notice boards, thus are not easily accessible to the applicants.

For the bicycle vendors, start-up consists of buying a bicycle and some 20-litre jerrycans to carry the water. They are not required to obtain a licence from the authorities. The backloaders only need to buy containers to start their business.

The main sources of funds for starting a business include remittances by family/ relatives (53 per cent), individual savings (34 per cent), retirement benefits (10 per cent), and micro-financing (3 per cent).

Starting a water kiosk is a significant undertaking so very few people do it. There is an upsurge of bicycle and backloaders, however, competing for the same customers.

The majority of bicycle vendors and backloaders incur high operating costs to keep repairing and replacing the plastic water containers they use. The kiosk owners have frequent pipeline repairs due to both vandalism and the poor quality of the plastic pipes used for such connections. The loose soil conditions also cause pipe bursts when soil comes loose during the rains or cracks during the dry season.

Competition for clients is increasing, causing the bicycle vendors and backloaders to sell water to neighbouring settlements like Komarock when they are experiencing shortages.

The challenges that face bicycle vendors and backloaders include frequent (justified and unjustified) harassment from city water authorities, police, and local administrators, as they do not have valid business licences to trade in water. There are no clearly laid down procedures or policies for allowing or inhibiting bicycle vendors and backloaders from operating. And because of this omission they are often harassed on the basis of hawking without a hawker's licence.

The water vending business is also erratic, being most lucrative during shortages. Hence those who operate kiosks also invest in storage facilities to take advantage of such situations. Unfortunately for the vendors, when water prices are at their peak (during shortages) they have to travel longer distances to get water and can only sell limited quantities.

A smaller number of small SWEs are employed by the wealthier SWEs, especially at water kiosks. The monthly salary varies between KSh1,800–5,400. The top of the range compares well with the minimum wage set by government, but the lower end is exploitative.

Water supply conflicts
There is much conflict during water shortages, as reported by 81 per cent of vendors and 63 per cent of kiosks.

7.5   SWOT analysis
The SWOT analysis to identify Strengths, Weaknesses, Opportunities and Threats for SWEs working in Maili Saba provided some useful insights, and the findings are summarized below.

7.6   Significance of SWEs (opportunities and constraints)
In the typical informal settlement of Maili Saba, 97 per cent of the water consumed is obtained from the utility. The users get their water from the kiosks, which are largely illegal and rarely pay for the water used. The kiosk owners pay for the connection fee and also provide their own pipes, sometime up to 3 km in length. This is a substantial investment. The utility has not laid any pipe infrastructure in the informal settlement. It can be concluded therefore that SWEs are a key player in the provision of water services in Maili Saba and similar informal settlements elsewhere in Nairobi, providing both the capital investment and also the operating costs.

Table 7.1. SWOT analysis	
Strengths	**Weaknesses**
• Majority (over 80%) of the SWEs live in Maili Saba. • The SWEs are young and literate. • SWEs provide necessary services. • SWEs provide alternative means of employment and livelihoods. • Kiosks provide over 90% of the water in Maili Saba. • There is a gender balance (50/50). • Most SWEs had been in the business for more than three years. • Kiosks operate on a full-time basis. • All kiosk operators obtain their supply from the utility.	• SWEs provide water of doubtful quality. • The distance between kiosks and the utility's main pipe varies from 1 to 3 km. • Licensing procedures are not transparent. • Capital costs to start SWE work are high. • Installation of pipelines is usually poor quality. • SWEs are harassed by the police and Nairobi City Council officials.
Opportunities	**Threats**
• NWSC has inadequate capacity to dialogue, hence is willing to work with partners. • There are good existing sector reforms. • Research team has done other similar work (WSP work in Kibera) so has wider knowledge of SWEs.	• The vendors are unwilling to participate in dialogue with NWSC for fear of the unknown. • NWSC might be unwilling to engage the SWEs in dialogue. • Vandalism is a problem.

The quality of the pipes and workmanship of SWE-installed infrastructure is poor, causing frequent leakages and high water losses. The water kiosks rarely pay their water bills, thus the utility incurs revenue losses.

It is worth noting that the utility is the primary and most important source of water, and the whole water system and supply chains rely on it.

The other bicycle vendors and backloaders provide a useful tertiary component in the whole water chain – but their volumes are low.

Constraints

The major constraints faced by the SWEs include:

Non-recognition by the utility. The utility does not recognize the SWEs as legitimate stakeholders who are providing an essential and necessary water delivery service to the informal settlements, where the utility cannot provide services as the settlements are not formally recognized by local authority's and central government's departments of physical planning.

Inadequate funding sources for capital investment. The SWEs currently obtain start-up or investment capital from family and individual savings, and in some cases retirement benefits are used. The formal banking sector cannot provide loans to help establish these businesses as both the business and the settlements are not formally recognized. There is however great business potential in this area, as there is little infrastructure (water and sanitation) in informal settlements and legalizing the SWEs, especially the kiosk owners, will encourage investment from the formal sector in this area.

Obscure (non-transparent) licensing procedures. The licensing procedures are long and shrouded in obscurity; the utility is now addressing and streamlining the process of issuing connections and licences in the informal settlements (there is a pilot scheme in Mukuru).

Frequent harassment by the police and utility security officers. With the pilot scheme testing the licensing process it is anticipated that the levels of harassment will reduce significantly.

Operating costs are high due to poor piping materials and poor workmanship. Operating costs for bicycle vendors are high due to frequent damage of the plastic containers and the need for bicycle repairs.

Gender. Woman vendors (who form the majority of the backloaders) endure specific difficulties due to harassment by their male counterparts especially during shortages.

Opportunities for SWEs

Market. There is a ready market in the informal settlements for the SWEs to engage in water delivery services.

Favourable political climate. The current political climate is conducive to advocating for and receiving recognition of the SWEs.

Utility. The utility, on its own initiative, is taking steps (pilot phase) to regularize the water supply to the informal settlements by proving meter chambers and streamlining billing and revenue collection. This is an opportunity for the SWEs to get licensed and engage in dialogue with the utility with ease. This is only a commercial endeavour, however, and these steps do not constitute legal recognition of the SWEs as agents of the utility; more support will be necessary to achieve this.

Collaboration. The utility is willing to engage with NGOs and CBOs to provide a service component to this initiative to benefit the residents of the informal settlements.

Chapter 8

Consumer perpectives on SWEs

8.1 Methodology and introduction

The opinions expressed in this chapter are based on key informant interviews at household level, focus group discussions and views expressed during the workshops.

The field survey interviewed a total of 66 respondents from the Mwengenye, Shilanga and Maili Saba informal settlements of Nairobi. The respondents were domestic users (86 per cent), food vendors (11 per cent), and construction sites (3 per cent). Figure 8.1 below shows the distribution of water consumers interviewed in three villages.

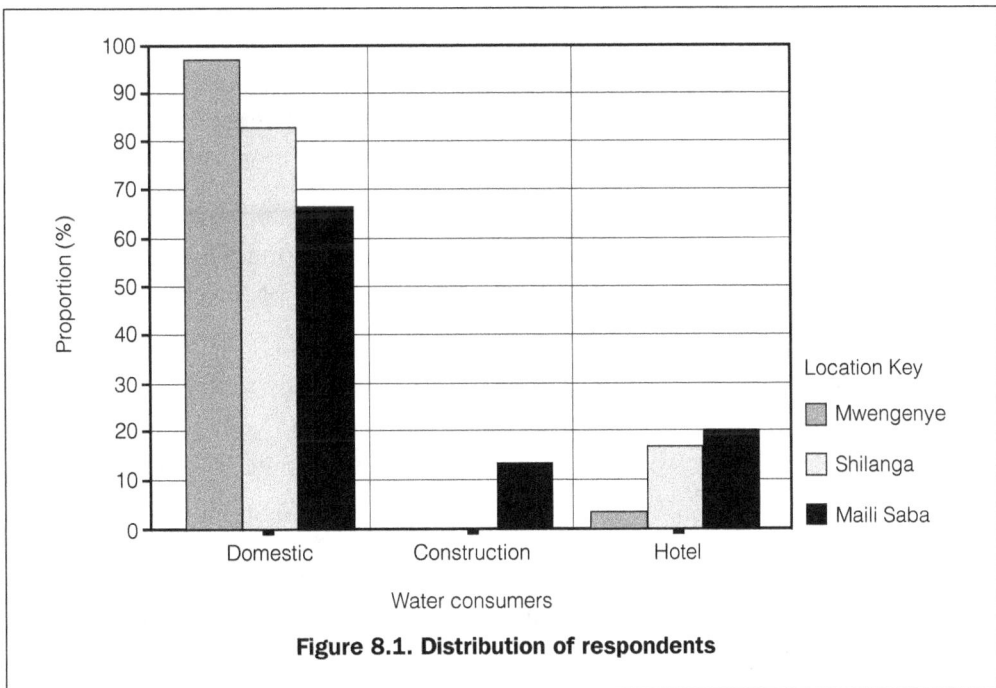

Figure 8.1. Distribution of respondents

The majority of respondents have settled in Maili Saba within the last 15 years. Of the users interviewed 77 per cent were female and 24 per cent were male. Only 2 per cent were under 18, 27 per cent were between 18 and 30, 36 per cent were 31 to 40, 18 per cent were 41 to 50 and 17 per cent were over 50. The figure below indicates the length of stay by the respondents in these areas.

The respondents were involved in either small businesses (61 per cent) or informal employment (39 per cent). The small businesses involved selling vegetables, running kiosks, and hand-crushing and selling gravel. Those in informal employment include home helps, watchmen, waiters and cooks. The average monthly income of respondents is KSh6,406 (US$84), or US$2.8 a day. Respondent households spent on average 9 per cent of their income on water.

Populations in the informal settlements are said to be a stable community as many of them have been there more than five years. They are able to engage in meaningful negotiations as many are literate. Poverty and lack of access to resources is a limiting factor, yet close to 10 per cent of their income is spent on water.

8.2   Water availability, reliability and convenience

The utility's supply is the main water supply in Maili Saba, providing over 97 per cent of the water in this settlement. Due to legal limitations (informal settlements are not recognized in law) the utility may not extend its network (formally) into the informal settlements. Of necessity therefore all utility pipe networks terminate or pass outside the informal settlements. This is why all the pipe networks into informal settlements are privately owned by small water enterprises whose owners mainly live within (80 per cent) the settlement and have recognized a business opportunity to supply water in the Maili Saba. Similar situations exist in other informal settlements.

There is therefore no link between the end-user (the respondents) and the utility. It is this scenario that shapes the views and perspectives of the end-users on the role and importance of the SWEs.

Water kiosks. The respondents considered water kiosks to be the key water service for their needs. During normal supply the kiosks provide a level of service that meets the expectations of the users as the queuing time is short, prices are reasonable, and the quality of the water is known and acceptable. During short supply this important water source is the one that is most affected and that in turn affects many users, causing sharp price increases and hardship to the users. Many respondents want individual yard connections, as shown by the 16 per cent who have water delivered despite the high premium.

In the meantime (and for the foreseeable future) water kiosks will remain the most important water supply option. Improving their management is probably the one most important factor that will have a positive impact on the water scenario in Maili Saba and other informal settlements in Nairobi. In Maili Saba, for instance, all kiosks are currently privately owned and operated. The respondents are of the view that introducing community-managed kiosks would provide the necessary competition to reduce prices and improve service. This option may attract necessary public sector resources to community groups for capital investment. This in our opinion may also trigger increased private investment (informal) as kiosks are a viable business for which loans may be given. Organizing the users into Water User's Associations, as provided for in the water policy, is a role that CBOs and NGOs like ITDG–EA (Practical Action) may have the scope to engage in.

The assumption is made here that the authorities will provide the necessary assurances that such informal settlements are given 'special planning status' in order to guarantee such investments.

The bicycle and back loaders. Vendors deliver water to households and other consumers at a much higher price – even during normal supply. That 16 per cent of users choose to buy their water this way points to the desire for a higher level of service to save the time of the household members who may be engaged in other income-generating activities. Some of the challenges facing this category of SWEs include mistrust of the water quality and high operating costs. They also suffer the double tragedy in that during short supply there is little water to sell and during normal supply households prefer to collect their own water. It is conceivable that this category of SWEs may lose if an improved working environment with more private/community kiosks is developed.

Quality of water. The water delivered by the utility is obtained from the same system that serves the rest of the city and is therefore assured to be of good quality. Despite the potential for local contamination between the utility mains and the kiosk, respondents consider the water to be of good quality. On the other hand the respondents do not know the source of the water that is delivered by the bicycle vendors and backloaders, who are prone to obtaining water from sources like open ponds and rivers and selling it at the same price as the water obtained from kiosks. When interviewed these vendors conceded that they do deliver low-quality water to constructions sites (which do not require high-quality water). This might be why users doubt the operations of the bicycle vendors and backloaders.

Reliability. In Maili Saba during normal supply water sells at an equivalent of US$1.25/m³ and users consider this cost reasonable. However during shortages the cost rises to close to US$3/m^3, causing real hardship to poor households. A regular supply (known quality and timing) is more desirable than a price reduction, as this helps stabilize prices. It also improves the quality, as the SWEs will have little need to go to other sources to supply the needs of their clients.

Relative importance of water uses. The largest market for SWEs is made up of households, and drinking water was rated as the highest need. Some 59 per cent of respondents boil drinking water. The cost of fuel (mainly charcoal) to boil water is an additional cost that the users can ill afford.

Domestic water uses were seen as the second most important. Those that use water for construction do so only to build, not as means of production like block or brick-making. Food vendors use water for productive purposes but are a small market for the SWEs.

Cost and ability to pay. The price of water collected from the water kiosks is on average US$1.25/m^3. This is 800 per cent more than the water tariff charged by the utility for water delivered through piped networks. (It is important to note that US$0.15/m^3 is the price of the delivered water while US$1.25/m^3 is what that water is then sold for.) A similar amount delivered by tertiary vendors to poor households costs up to 2,000 per cent more. It is against this background that users consider the price of water to be high. The opportunity cost of time spent collecting water has forced some of these poor households (16 per cent) to pay the extra for residential water delivery.

Whereas affluent consumers in the formal settlements pay their water bills after receiving the water, in the informal settlements residents have to pay before receiving their water, thus requiring them to have cash at all times when they collect water. This limits their water consumption and forces them to resort to sources of doubtful quality. The respondents were unanimous that they would accept the inflated price of US$1.25/m^3 if they got in return a reliable, convenient and improved water supply even when short of cash.

8.3   Other important considerations

Water management and governance issues

Water distribution networks. The respondents are aware that the network in the informal settlement is privately owned and operated by the SWEs. They recognize therefore that these SWEs (kiosk owners/operators) are providing the necessary capital investment to increase water distribution, even though they charge a high tariff for the service. As more SWEs join the market or existing SWEs seek to increase their selling points, (some SWEs sell water at different points within the settlements), the users benefit from reduced queuing time and distances at the waterpoints.

Community efforts. Some community members have formed groups in order to engage in water businesses in the same way as the SWEs. The success of such groups has been limited because of the high investment costs needed, poor entrepreneurial skills, and heavy bureaucracy at the utility, among other things. It is not clear what benefits such groups could offer as SWEs and it may be that their niche might be in organizing the users to lobby the utility to control /regularize the tariffs charged by the SWEs to the end-users.

Community groups are another useful entry point to advocate for improved behaviour and hygiene practices, especially in handling water and sanitation.

The respondents recognize the inherent weakness of community-organized groups as currently organized, and that they will require strengthening in order to engage with other processes like the Local Authority Service Delivery Action Plan (LASDAP).

Gender roles in water supply. The responsibility for water collection and management at household level rests with the female members of the household. They decide when and where to buy water, but the means to buy are vested in the head of the household (who may also be female). Any proposed improvements to the SWE system will need to seek their views in order to tailor the interventions to suit this important segment of the community.

Water, sanitation, and health. The respondents have a clear understanding of the relationship between clean water, proper wastewater disposal, proper hygiene behaviour, and good health.

Chapter 9

Relationship between Utilities and SWEs

9.1 Constraints faced by SWEs

This SWE research project aims to identify the constraints and opportunities available for investment in small-scale water provision either by water vendors or kiosk owners. Following discussions with various utility managers (official positions and personal opinions about small water enterprises in Nairobi's informal settlements), a number of facts were captured in relation to the wider water services sector. Following is a summary of issues linked to the water sector and SWEs in particular.

9.2 Ministry of Water and Irrigation

The function of the ministry overall is policy formulation, legislation and guidance. It speaks through the policies and through the Water Act.

The current policy (Sessional Paper No.1 of 1999) provides for the participation of the users and private sector in the development and management of the sector. Users may participate through the formation of Water User Associations or community self-help groups.

The private sector participation envisaged is usually of large formal organizations. However in the current political climate and given the recent remarks by the minister – who alluded to the need to address the problem of water vendors (mainly tanker operators) who serve the more affluent parts of the city and are alleged to collude with each other to cause artificial shortages in order to increase their business – the government is committed to improving the services that citizens receive, including those living in informal settlements. With this prevailing positive political climate, advocating for the recognition of SWEs in view of the important role they are playing in the water sector is likely to yield positive and lasting impacts and outcomes.

The SWEs who operate mainly in the informal settlements have received little attention at the ministerial level, despite the fact that they engage in activities (selling water) that have a direct impact on a large segment of the urban (Nairobi) population.

The current water sector reforms are opening windows of opportunity for the role of SWEs to be recognized.

9.3   Nairobi City Water and Sewerage Company

The Nairobi City Water and Sewerage Company was born of the former Nairobi City Water and Sewerage Department in response to the on-going water sector reforms which required the privatization or commercialization of water service delivery.

This trend of transforming such departments into private companies has been done in Nairobi, Kisumu, Eldoret and Nyeri, among other towns. Towns like Mombasa, who relied on the National Water Conservation and Pipeline Corporation, have either to create their own companies from start or allow in external private companies.

The Company has been in existence for a few months, and commendable efforts can be recognized from the plans that are in place in piloting innovative approaches in 15 villages and informal settlements along the Lunga Lunga, Outering, Mombassa and Enterprise Roads. The informal settlements include Mukuru (Kwa Njenga, Kwa Reuben, Kingston, Fuata Nyayo, Marigo-ini, Kisii and Kayaba) among others. Mukuru is one of the largest slum areas and interventions here are likely to result in significant reduction in water losses and to increase revenue.

The primary purpose of the Company is to reduce water losses and to increase revenue collection. To achieve this dual objective the company has recognized that the rampant illegal connections coupled with inadequate metering was a major contributor to the high level of unaccounted-for water in the city of Nairobi.

Until now small water enterprises connected to the utility pipeline haphazardly. Now the utility has taken two major steps:

First, all existing and future connections will be centralized through a valve chamber where the utility pipe will terminate or provide a tee to accommodate at least 25 meter connections in one chamber. The chamber will be locked to secure the meters and the connections. Each connection will be fitted with a stopcock after the meter to facilitate repairs and maintenance. This action will ensure that only legal connections are allowed and that because the metering is done close to the utility pipeline all leakages are a loss to the SWE and not the utility. The SWEs also provide a deposit of KSh1,500 that is used to offset any payment default and the utility is strict in enforcing disconnections.

The second action is that all bills for a particular chamber/box (set of connections) are delivered periodically to a central place where the SWEs are expected to come and settle them. Any bill that remains unsettled for 40 days risks disconnection, which is effected promptly. These two actions might be interpreted to mean recognition of SWEs by the utility. Admittedly, the two actions greatly improve the working environment of the SWEs and reduce the risk of harassment of SWEs by the regular security operatives, and so are a necessary step, but they do not constitute formal recognition of SWEs by the utility.

There are a few things to note:

- The meter chamber (box) is located outside the informal settlements.

- The piping between the chamber and the kiosks is the responsibility of the SWEs, who continue to use the same poor materials and workmanship.

- The utility has not provided resources (neither money nor skills) to support the SWEs.

The utility has no plans in the immediate future to move into informal settlements. This is understandable considering that the utility would require formal way leaves/ passages, a condition that would be difficult to achieve in the unplanned informal settlements. The greatest hurdle to achieving meaningful engagement by the utility in informal settlements is the lack of legal recognition by the planning authorities – City Council, Physical Planning Department – of the informal settlements. The planning authority needs to declare these settlements 'Special Planning Areas' to facilitate service provision by the utilities.

Currently, the kiosks are privately owned and are the only way that residents of informal settlements receive water from the utilities.

The SWEs are neither licensed nor appointed as agents by the utility. They receive no material or technical support and are currently not recognized as providing a useful and essential services to the residents in the informal settlements.

The utility is willing to work in partnership with willing CBOs and NGOs to identify and pilot innovative approaches that will improve the status of the SWEs and improve the level of service to the end users. These interventions may include extending the pipe network (improved materials/ workmanship) and establishing meter chambers/boxes within the settlements, encouraging users to organize into

Water User Associations, providing micro-credit, and linking water supply to adequate sanitation (human /wastewater, disposal) and hygienic behaviour change among other things.

It would therefore be of benefit to the SWEs for them to organize themselves into a legal body to be able to engage with the utility to a level where they can receive support. The consumers are the ultimate beneficiaries and here lies a huge opportunity for CBOs and NGOs to engage for resource mobilization.

The current scenario provides an opportunity for Phase 2 and the research project to engage with the utility in its 'Informal Improvements' project to support the utility.

- Learn and systematize the lessons.

- Bring to the fore issues relating to resolving equity problems, that is how to allocate the kiosks to existing kiosks owners and how new kiosks will be allocated.

- Support SWEs to overcome constraints.

- Sensitize and mobilize users to engage positively with the utility.

9.4   Nairobi City Council

Nairobi City Council, in recognizing the dilemma of informal settlements in applying and obtaining water using the standard requirements, which include plot number, has made special provisions through a Council Resolution to allow applicants from informal settlements to receive connections. However, the by-laws have not been changed to reflect this council resolution.

Chapter 10

Consensus-building for Partnerships

10.1 Background

Most people living in informal settlements are excluded from conventional utility services and have to rely on SWEs for their water supply. In recognition of the role played by SWEs in fulfilling the water supply needs of Kenya's urban settlements, the research involved several categories of players in the water sector – namely water users, water vendors, and the water utilities – to identify the constraints and opportunities and to test the strategies for enabling SWEs to deliver an acceptable water service to the poor urban dwellers of Nairobi. Maili Saba was selected as the research area (see Chapter 5).

Discussions were also held with several different utilities to explore opportunities for SWEs within the context of the policy guidelines and institutional frameworks of the major actors.

To review and compare the findings, a stakeholders' workshop was organized, bringing together the SWEs, Nairobi City Council, The Nairobi City Water and Sewerage Company Ltd, the Ministry of Water Resources Management and Development, and various NGOs and consumers. The SWEs included kiosk owners, bicycle vendors and back/headloaders.

10.2 Workshop proceedings

Introduction

To use the time available efficiently for the specific tasks, the forum adopted the following structure for discussion:

Presentation of research findings

The principal researchers (Isaack Oenga and David Kuria) presented their research findings to the workshop. This was followed by a short presentation by the ministry giving the highlights of the policy guidelines and the current status of the reform process. NWSC provided its overview of the way forward as the company prepares to go into full operations, while the NGOs present gave some highlights of their work in the informal settlement areas.

The discussions explored links between the SWEs and the national water development goals, the utilities, and policy and institutional issues in the water sector.

Small water enterprises (SWEs)

The water vendors earn their livelihoods from their business and feel the company should involve them in formulating any guidelines that aim to streamline the sector. They are apprehensive that although individual connections are important and are the ultimate goal, in the meantime SWEs should be considered somewhere in the supply and distribution chain. They asked the company to categorically define how they will create a balance between individual connections and SWEs' roles in the supply.

The SWEs suggested that if the company is going to do away with them, them there should be a compensation plan, since some of them took out loans to make their initial investments. But they were strongly behind the alternative suggestion that they be licensed to operate as distributors and be supplied with the water and the appropriate connection standards. This will guarantee the continuity of their livelihoods and the supply of the community at large.

Ministry of Water & Irrigation (MWI)

The ministry's target is for individual households to have connections and be served with clean piped water. But this is not feasible in the short term, so the intermediate strategic plan is to improve access to water services. Accessibility in this context is about reducing the national average distance to a water source to 2 km. The Maili Saba area fits well in the accessibility plan, just like any other region in the country. Taking the Nairobi situation, there is the potential to reduce the distance travelled by individuals to the nearest water source to an average of 5 m. (The situation in Maili Saba at the moment is 250 m.)

This vision is for planned settlements with potential water consumers and demand and wastewater management systems – criteria that Maili Saba meets. It is among the very few informal settlements in Nairobi that have received special planning status – they are only waiting for formalization of the plan by the relevant authorities.

The ministry is also concerned with the lack of professional commitment in the way water utilities address water supply issues. Of particular concern is the failure by service providers to provide information and advice to water users and SWEs about water supplies. MWI recognizes the important role played by the water kiosks in the country and encourages their involvement in the water supply and distribution chain.

Nairobi City Water and Sewerage Company Limited (NWSC)

Overview

The Nairobi City Water and Sewerage Company Ltd came into being as a result of the implementation of the Water Act, which commercialized the water sector. The company has inherited several management and technical problems from the Nairobi City Council Water and Sewerage Department. The first obstacle the company has to overcome is to address the water distribution problems that currently affect the entire city, for example, the Eastland's area has more water than Upper Nairobi. The strategy is to improve the distribution, thereby improving the whole network. A pump has indeed been installed to shift excess water to areas of low supply.

There is also the challenge of standardizing the materials currently being used in the water supply distribution network. Poor materials have led to poor distribution because of water loss along the service lines.

The NWSC has neither the competence nor the capacity to undertake community consultation processes and would welcome support in this regard.

Situation in informal settlements

The Water Board has put together a team to assess the possibility of bulk metering in an effort to help monitor the amount of water supplied to particular areas. This will go a long way towards making the water supply agent more responsible.

Kiosks sprang from what used to be 'group development and reticulation' systems. Most informal settlements have no formal building and planning system, so the kiosks appeared. The immediate priority is to dialogue with kiosk owners and other SWEs about the best way to improve their services to the residents. NWSC is willing and ready to work with residents through organized groups. The challenge therefore is for the SWEs to organize themselves and speak with one voice. This is the right time for all the stakeholders to air their views, which will go a long way towards serving the company's vision of water for all. The Water Company recognizes that the task of streamlining the sector is enormous. They inherited several problems from the City Council and therefore the Water Board, which is mandated to work on the policy guidelines, needs a working partnership with all the other stakeholders.

Commitment

The Nairobi City Water and Sewerage Company Ltd is keen to establish a customer-friendly working environment. They want an environment where the water vendors (especially kiosk owners) in the informal settlements are encouraged to regularize their operations, pay their water bills, and strengthen mechanisms for reducing water losses due to leakage and unpaid bills.

The company will encourage their staff to properly identify themselves in future, in order to discourage fraudsters who pretend to be representing the company. The utilities were urged to regulate the water supply and distribution systems to protect all consumers. Water users must also be protected in terms of water pricing, quality and reliability of supply. The company will continuously work with all the stakeholders, and especially the SWEs, to deliver quality service to its customers.

Capacity building

The workshop emphasized the need for community capacity building. In order to achieve NWSC's desire to dialogue with communities, mobilization and involvement will be necessary. Procedures and processes for such an engagement with informal settlement communities will need to be developed in a participative and interactive process.

It was recognized that the NWSC has expressed goodwill by resolving to involve the community groups in the water supply operations. Unfortunately there is no clear commitment to involve them in solving the sanitation problems.

Adequacy of bulk water supply

The chronic water leakages in Nairobi undermine the bulk water supply and the viability of the whole water and sanitation systems. Immediate and urgent measures are necessary to address this aspect of the water and sanitation services. Solving the problem will means addressing issues such as consumer's perspective, public attitudes, physical improvements of the physical components – especially the aging distribution system – and staff attitude, competencies and loyalty.

Way forward

The workshop made the following recommendations:

- The sector needs to carry out the measures and processes necessary to involve all stakeholders – and especially customers and actors like SWEs – who live and work in the informal settlements. These informal settlements are home to more than 60 per cent of the population of Nairobi.

- Decisions on equitable water supply for both present and future are a responsibility which should be properly exercised with the participation of the whole community.

- Mechanisms need to be evolved to assure community inputs in the decision-making and implementation processes.

Market structure issues

Just as large-scale investors are encouraged by the sector management to bid for the investment opportunities, income-generating activities for low-income areas with strong linkages with water supply should be considered for similar encouragement.

SWE consultation should feature strongly in any regulatory process aimed at streamlining the sector, such as licensing process and simplification of the tariff type approval process.

Any restrictive policy on the licensing of operations by any category of SWE could deny the people in the informal settlements from creating income-generating initiatives.

The introduction of community management groups to run water services could need to include individual-run kiosks so as to diversify management options, while subjecting all these options to fair rules and regulations.

Mechanisms need to be developed to engage SWEs in a progress of organizing, recognizing and regulating these services through, for instance, the formation of SWE associations or groups.

The stakeholders should work towards an improved information-sharing strategy among the users, SWEs and the company. This will create awareness on various policy issues, including legislation and guidelines regarding water resource development.

Chapter 11

Conclusions and Recommendations

Phase 1 of the 'Better Access to Water in Informal Settlements through Support to Small Water Enterprises' research project was conducted in Maili Saba, an informal settlement in north-eastern Nairobi. It has a population of about 10,000 people, most of whom derive their livelihoods from small businesses and informal employment. The average monthly income is US$70 per month, 10 per cent of which is spent on water. Maili Saba is a typical informal settlement, and is a fair representation of the larger informal unplanned settlements of Nairobi.

11.1 Key findings
- The residents of Maili Saba receive over 97 per cent of their water from the utility mains.

- All the water from the utility is sold through water kiosks.

- Over 70 per cent of the residents collect their water from the kiosks, while 16 per cent depend on the services of the bicycle vendors or backloaders to deliver water to their households.

- The cost to the kiosk of utility water is US$0.15/m^3, which they sell at US$1.25/m^3. When delivered directly to the household (through bicycle vendors or headloaders) the cost of water rises to US$5/m^3 during normal supply. Short supply causes high price increases and it can be concluded that reliability of supply is crucial to the stability of the tariffs charged.

- The users consider the utility water to be good quality, while other sources are considered to be of doubtful quality.

The SWEs (kiosks) face the following challenges:

- Inadequate funding sources to finance capital investment

- Inadequate capital base

- Non-recognition by the utility and other regulating bodies

- Poor piping materials and workmanship

- High operating costs

- High bureaucracy at the utility

The kiosks play a very significant role, as they are the sole link between the utility and the residents of Maili Saba in the supply if water. Improvements in the working environment will greatly benefit these SWEs and will enhance the reliability of the water supply in Maili Saba. This will in turn increase the level of service and stabilize the water charges.

The bicycle vendors and backloaders might be considered opportunistic and may lose business in an improved working environment. The utility has little incentive to engage with this category. The kiosk is a viable business capable of creating regular employment for the owner.

The users want improved services delivery within their means. The NWSC is also keen to reduce water wasted through leaks and illegal connections, improve its revenue collection, and deliver a higher level of service to its customers. Improved piped networks will mean that more kiosks can be developed, which will reduce distances and increase water supply. The kiosks also offer a higher return both to the NWSC and the individuals running them, and a better service to the tertiary vendors and customers. The utility will require support in capacity building, especially in the areas of community mobilization and organization, as well as in training staff in the participatory management of the water facilities.

The utility is engaged in a pilot project aimed at improving the public image of the company and developing good will. The informal settlements projects being piloted in the Mukuru informal settlements are aimed at reducing water losses, improving revenue collection, regularizing connections (some were illegal), and streamlining the procedures for obtaining connections at the utility offices.

It is important to note that the utility mains terminate outside the informal settlements in a meter chamber. All the pipelines into the informal settlement are installed by the kiosks owners, despite their limited capital.

Overall reform in the water sector embraces the concept of partnerships with the various stakeholders in the water sector. Commercialisation of the water supply service has been accepted and is being implemented.

The apparent disadvantage to the backloaders and bicycle vendors will hopefully be compensated by increased income-generating opportunities brought about by increased water supply to the areas. These include but are not limited to poultry-rearing (which employs help), jobs at new and busier kiosks, and the fact that households will buy more water as the costs drop, thus requiring the services of the backloaders and bicycle vendors.

SWEs are crucial stakeholders in delivering water services to informal settlements. And the utility is now willing to regularize them and is seeking ways to improve the working relationship with the SWEs. Users in informal settlements rely largely on the utility water supply but access is solely through the kiosks. Improving the working environment for SWEs will have direct benefits for the users.

The SWEs lack the necessary capital technical skills and entrepreneur management skills to ensure viability in their business. This affects the whole water supply delivery.

There is scope for Phase 2 to address the constraints and harness opportunities to improve the working environment for SWEs, and to support the utility to achieve its mandate of delivery of water to the residents of Nairobi without excluding the informal settlements.

The test hypothesis is to develop a joint partnership approach where the water utility – within the overall policy framework – supports and improves the reticulation systems and then engages the SWEs to operate them.

11.2   Opportunities for Phase 2

The current scenario offers opportunities for Phase 2 to pilot, develop and implement the interventions assessed as being the most likely to succeed. The interventions will seek to improve water services for the residents of the informal settlement (Mukuru) where the utility is undertaking a pilot intervention.

ITDG–EA (Practical Action) will partner with WEDC and the utility to test the most feasible interventions.

The most feasible interventions include:

1.   **Physical improvement:** To pilot and test a piped network that takes water from the current utility meter chambers into the informal settlement. The improved network will provide meter chambers within the settlement, managed by the SWEs. The SWEs will work with consumers to plan a water pipe route that will provide the most advantages to SWEs and users.

This pilot will include provision of bulk meters at the current utility meter chamber and also individual meters within the settlement chamber. This will assist in monitoring water losses that might occur in the pipelines.

The improved network will have the following benefits:

- Improved water supply in the informal settlement

- An opportunity for the utility to test new management methods and physical improvements in informal settlements

- Opportunities for SWEs and users to engage in a shared vision for improving water supply in the settlement

2. **Strengthening SWEs:** Phase 2 of the project will develop, test and pilot organizing the SWEs into cooperatives in order to engage with the utility with one voice. The SWEs will be encouraged and supported to form cooperative societies that will engage with the utility and other stakeholders.

This will also provide the SWEs with the opportunity to seek and receive credit from formal lending institutions. The utility will also be encouraged to pilot financing mechanisms, where it provides materials to the SWEs and recovers the costs from the sales of water.

3. **Capacity building:** The utility will receive support to document and systematize lesson learning from its current interventions and also from the Phase 2 inputs.

4. **User organization:** The primary purpose of this input is to support attitude change to reduce vandalism and encourage a positive dialogue between users and other stakeholders.

The current water sector reforms offer ample opportunities for positive engagement and lesson learning that can be a stimulus in way that the utility operates. The lessons will also offer the evidence for policy dialogue, as it is policy that is being put into operation in Kenya and in the region.

References

Albu, M. and Njiru, C. (2002) 'The role of small-scale providers in urban areas'. *Waterlines* Vol.20 No.3, pp16-18.

Alder, G. (1995) 'Tackling poverty in Nairobi's informal settlements: Developing an institutional strategy', *Environment and Urbanization*, Vol.7 No.2, pp85-108.

AMREF and GoK (1997) 'The second participatory assessment study - Kenya Vol.1'. Office of the Vice- president and Ministry of Planning and National Development, Nairobi.

Ashley, C. and Carney, D. (1999) *Sustainable Livelihoods: Lessons form early experience*. Department for International Development (DFID), London.

Bakker, K. (2003) 'A political ecology of water privatization', *Studies in Political economy*, Issue 70, May 2003, pp35-58.

BER (1999) *Kibera Settlement Alternative Water Management Arrangements*, Business and Economics Research Co. Ltd. Final Report, Vol.1, Main report. Business and Economic Research Co. Ltd., Nairobi, Kenya, December, 1999.

BER (1997) *Study of Public Water Points (Kiosks) in Kibera, Nairobi*, Business and Economics Research, Nairobi, Kenya.

Bosire, O. (2002) *Assessment of local service delivery within informal and peri-urban settlements in Kenya*. Matrix Development Consultants Report.

Collignon, B. and Vezina, M. (2000) *Independent water and sanitation providers in African cities: full report of a ten-country study*. Water and Sanitation Programme, World Bank and IRC.

Etherington, A., Wicken, J. and Bajracharya, D. (2002) 'Preparing for Private Sector Management of Kathmandu Urban Water Supply'. WaterAid, Nepal, 2002.

GoK (2003a) *National Development Plan 2003-2008.* Government of Kenya, Nairobi.

GoK (2003b) *Economic recovery strategy for wealth and employment creation 2003-2007.* Government of Kenya, Nairobi.

GoK and UNCHS (2002) 'Nairobi situation analysis consultative report'. Government of Kenya and United Nations Centre for Human Settlements (Habitat) Collaborative Nairobi Slum Upgrading Initiative.

GoK (2002) *The Water Act 2002.* Kenya Gazette Supplement No.107 (Acts No.9), Part III section 7(1). Government of Kenya, Nairobi.

GoK (2000) 'Workshop report on national water policy as it relates to poverty alleviation held at KCCT Mbagathi, February 2-4, 2000'. Ministry of Environment and Water Resources.

GoK (2000a) 'Review of the water supply and sanitation sector: Aide Memoire'. Joint World Bank, KfW, GTZ and AFD Mission.

GoK (2000b) *Interim Poverty Reduction Strategy Paper, 2002-2003.* Government of Kenya, Nairobi. <http://www.imf.org/external/NP/prsp/2000/ken/01/INDEX.HTM> [20 Dec 2005]

GoK (1999) *Sessional Paper No.1 of 1999 on National Policy on Water Resources Management.* Government of Kenya, Nairobi.

GoK and JICA (1992) *The Study on National Water Master Plan: Water Resources Development and Use Plan Towards 2010. Main Report Vol. 1.* Ministry of Water Development, prepared with the assistance of Japan International Cooperation Agency (JICA).

Hardoy, J., Mitlin, D. and Satterthwaite, D. (2001) *Environmental Problems in Third World Cities.* Earthscan Publications Ltd, London.

Harper, M. (2000) *Public Services Through Private Enterprise: Micro-privatisation for improved delivery.* ITDG Publications, London.

Howard Humphreys and Partners (1996) *Third Nairobi Water Supply Project. Short-term plan to 1995.* Consultancy Report, Nairobi.

IRC (1996) 'Developments in water, sanitation and environment', *Water Newsletter* No. 245. International Water and Sanitation Centre, WHO Collaborating Centre, 1996.

Kariuki, M., Gikaru, L. Musumba, B. and Mbuvi, J. (2000) 'The water kiosks of Kibera', Field note. Water and Sanitation Program, East and Southern Africa Region, the World Bank.

Lewis , M.A. and Miller, T.R. (1987) 'Public–private partnerships in water supply and sanitation in Sub-Saharan Africa', *Health Policy and Planning*, Vol 2 No.1, pp70-79.

Maji na Ufanisi (2002) *Poverty reduction and water access in Sub-Saharan Africa - Kenya case study.* WaterAid and ODI.

Moriarty, P. (2002) 'Sustainable Livelihoods Approaches: An explanation', *Waterlines* Vol 20 No.3, pp.4–6.

Nicol, A. (2000) *Adopting a sustainable livelihoods approach to water projects: implications for policy and practice.* Working Paper 133. Overseas Development Institute, London.

Nipon Koei Co. Ltd (1999) 'The Aftercare Study on the National Water Master Plan in the Republic of Kenya. JICA Draft Final Report'. Consultancy Report, Nairobi.

Njoroge, B. and Obel-Lawson, E. (eds) (2000) *Small-scale independent providers of water and sanitation to the urban poor: A case of Nairobi, Kenya.* Water and Sanitation Programme, UNDP-World Bank.

Obel-Lawson, E., and Njoroge, B.K. (1999) *Small service providers make a big difference,* Field note No 5. Water and Sanitation Programme, the World Bank.

Plummer, J. and Gentry, B. (2002) 'Establishing Appropriate Organisational and Contractual Arrangements', Chapter 8 in *Focusing Partnerships: A sourcebook for municipal capacity building in public-private partnerships* (Editor, J. Plummer). Earthscan, London.

Sanderson, D. (2000) 'Cities, disasters and livelihoods', *Environment and Urbanization*, Vol 12 No.2, pp93-102.

Solo, Tova Maria (1998) 'Competition in Water and Sanitation: The role of small-scale entrepreneurs'. *Public Policy Journal,* Issue 165, Private Sector Development, the World Bank, Washington DC.

Solo, T.M. (2000) 'Independent water entrepreneurs in Latin America; the other private sector in water services' (draft). World Bank, Washington DC.

Solo, T.M. (1999) 'Small-scale entrepreneurs in urban water and sanitation market', *Environment and Urbanization*, Vol.11 No.1, pp117-131.

Stephens, C. (1996) 'Healthy cities or unhealthy islands? The health and social implications of urban inequality', *Environment and Urbanization* Vol 8 No.2, pp.9-30.

Syagga, P.M. (2001) *Integrated, multi-sectoral and sectoral urban development initiatives in Kenya.* Working Paper 2, The Schumacher Centre for Technology and Development, Rugby, United Kingdom.

Thompson, J., Porras, I.T., Wood, E., Tumwine, J.K., Mujwahuzi, M.R., Katui-Katua, M., and Johnstone, N. (2000) 'Waiting at the Tap: Changes in urban water use in East Africa over three decades', *Environment and Urbanization* Vol.12 No.2, pp.37-52.

UN-HABITAT (2002) 'A Rapid Economic Appraisal of Rents in Slums and Informal Settlements' Working document, UN-HABITAT, Nairobi, Kenya.

UN-Habitat (2003) *Water and Sanitation in the World's Cities: Local action for global goals.* Earthscan Publications, London.

UNCHS (1997) 'Analysis of data and global urban indicators database'. UNCHS Urban Indicators Programme, Phase 1994-6, Nairobi.

Van Doorne, J.H. (1985) *A Review of Small-scale Irrigation Schemes in Kenya.* FAO, Rome.

World Bank (2000) *Services to the Urban Poor Small Providers Make a Big Difference in East Africa.* Water and Sanitation Program, World Bank.

Appendix 1

Overview

This project proposal is a mitigation effort aimed at creating workable strategies for the participation of small water enterprises (SWEs) in the provision and supply of reliable, affordable and safe water to poor residents of urban informal settlements in Nairobi. The project idea was derived from the findings of research funded by UK Department for International Development (DFID) and carried out by the Water, Engineering and Development Centre (WEDC) at Loughborough University, UK in collaboration with a local partner, Practical Action – East Africa (formerly ITDG – East Africa).

The primary theme of the study was to investigate constraints, opportunities, and strategies for enabling small water enterprises (SWEs) to play a more significant role, together with local government authorities, utilities and public agencies, in improving access to water by low-income residents of urban informal settlements.

The primary data were collected from the residents and SWEs in Maili Saba informal settlement, while secondary information was derived from an extensive literature review.

Critical analysis of the current role of SWEs and value chains clearly illustrates a strong need to enhance the SWEs' effort to fill a gap in the water supply. Key stakeholders concede that it is important within the current water reform framework strategy to engage in this process.

Main goal
The main goal of this intervention is to improve the well-being of the poor in urban informal settlements through improved water supply services. This will happen by establishing a partnership between the SWEs and the utility to increase accessibility to safe, affordable and reliable water.

Proposed intervention

Maili Saba, the research site for Phase 1, is a typical informal settlement and has yielded useful insights into the relationships between the SWEs, the utility, the relevant government departments, and consumers. Phase 2 of the research process will be undertaken in Mukuru – a large informal settlement where the utility has now taken the initiative to pilot initiatives to reduce water losses and improving revenue collection.

Phase 2 of the research project will conduct action research to pilot, develop and implement at least two interventions that are most likely to succeed. These interventions will seek to improve water services for the urban poor who rely on SWEs to deliver water. SWEs will be encouraged to take up these new opportunities, while the utility will be encouraged to recognize SWEs' potential to provide and support the provision of water services to informal settlements currently not served directly by the utility. The major interventions will include:

• SWEs' associations or cooperatives – Support to the SWEs and the users – currently the SWEs operate individually and do not have a common voice or approach to business. The project will organize the SWEs (especially the kiosk owners) to form an association or cooperative in order to enhance their recognition. This will have several advantages. First, the association will have a position from which to enter into dialogue with the utility and the financing institutions from a credible platform. Second, it will be easier to apply to the utility for support in technical support and materials in order to improve both the workmanship and quality of construction materials used in the infrastructure. Third, the association could apply to serve certain specific areas in the settlements, and thus obtain a term licence that can be used as collateral in securing loans and other services.

In practice, a major element of supporting SWEs lies in creating an operating environment that protects them from harassment and extortion. Recognizing and regularizing their role at utility level will help reduce rent-seeking opportunities, at least by officials.

A need for 'capacity building' initiatives for SWEs is identified as a way of making SWEs organize themselves and voice their needs and concerns. Other incentives relevant to SWEs may include:

• Support for accessing micro-credit (e.g. group facilitation and information)

• Leasing of transport equipment and vending facilities

- Rental of secure premises for storing equipment

- Management (operation and maintenance) of water supply points

SWEs will be supported to improve their business, quality of water, and reliable delivery and use of appropriate technologies for improved water supply and delivery.

The SWEs will also build capacity to manage their own organizations and encourage the effective use of technology.

- **User associations** – The users will be encouraged to engage with the SWEs and/or organize into user groups in order to apply for communal water kiosks, and so extend services to those areas in the informal settlements that are currently underserved.

  There will be a positive collaboration forged between SWEs with the community and all stakeholders to encourage price control, water quality and regulation during shortages. The community will also be engaged in value-added water management initiatives.

- **Physical improvements** – The current utility pilot project is focused on improving revenue collection and reducing water losses. The meter chambers are outside the informal settlements. The project will pilot the improving and extending of the piped network into the settlements. Priority will be given to those areas that are currently underserved.

- **The utility initiatives** will be studied closely to draw lessons that the utility could use to scale up the interventions to other areas. Collaboration between the research team (ITDG-EA (Practical Action), the utility, the SWEs, and the users) will provide learning opportunities for scaling up. The interventions will be undertaken in close consultation with the utility to ensure that the relevant concerns and questions are addressed in order to assure a practical approach to solving existing concerns and testing workable solutions. The Nairobi City Water and Sewerage Company has embarked on reducing water losses and increasing revenue in fifteen (15) informal settlements on a pilot basis along the Nairobi rivers. The main intervention is to provide central meter chambers at appropriate locations near informal settlements and to regularize all the connections. This intervention will achieve a reduction in leakages and increased revenue.

Expected outcomes

It is expected that these interventions will achieve:

- a conducive environment is which SWEs are recognized as an integral component of the water supply chain in the Mukuru informal settlement and in the city of Nairobi in general;

- improved water supply and reduced water shortages;

- improved quality of life for the residents and in particular women and children; and

- lessons for wider sharing in the Kenyan water sector and beyond.

Appendix 2

Logframe Summary

Narrative summary	Objective verifiable indicators (OVI)	Means of verification (MOV)	Important assumptions
Goal: To develop an efficient water supply system model and strategies in poor urban informal settlements	Delivery of affordable, safe reliable water to poor urban settlement Community support and partnership with SWEs	• Cost of water • Quality of water supplies • Community water management programme	The current positive climate will prevail in the water sector and in the utility
Purpose: To establish and strengthen partnerships for better accessibility to safe, affordable and reliable water in poor urban informal settlements	Establishment of functional SWEs Formal arrangements with Nairobi Water Supply Company (NWSC) Improved capacity to manage and plan water delivery and use	• Inventory of SWEs in the area • Licence from NWSC	SWEs' willingness to foster partnerships
Outputs: Modelling appropriate water supply partnerships for improved accessibility	Formation of Water User Associations and SWE association Official licensing and partnership formalization with NWSC	• Workable supply chain • Registration with appropriate agencies and licensing	SWEs' commitment to develop partnership

(Table A6.1. continued on next page)

Appendices

Table A6.1.   Working with SWEs towards improved access to water by the urban poor *(continued)*

Narrative summary	Objective verifiable indicators (OVI)	Means of verification (MOV)	Important assumptions
Strengthened capacity to manage and sustain small water enterprises (SWEs)	Functional partnerships and value based linkages between SWEs, NWSC & Community Reliable safe water supplies Capacity building for better customer service, Business planning, Hygiene concerns & general water management	• Associations programmes and business plans • Handling of community concerns • Governance issues	SWEs' need for capacity development and improvement of service delivery
Foster linkages of SWEs within the ongoing water reform programme	Link SWEs and reposition them within the reform programme and structure Participation in the wider reform and service delivery networks Improved accessibility to resources for better water delivery (like Water Trust Fund, or LASDAP)	• Linkages with NWSC and other related water management programmes • Capacity development within the Association	Maintained collaboration between SWEs and other government and non-governmental agencies
Improved social delivery system through SWEs	Enhance community water use awareness campaigns, hygiene, waste water management and sanitation	• Community participation in water management programmes	Community support and goodwill
Improved information sharing and documentation of best practices	Documented case studies on the utility–SWE partnerships and service improvement	• Records and other information gathered	Disposition towards continuous improvement

(Table A6.1. continued on next page)

Table A6.1.	Working with SWEs towards improved access to water by the urban poor *(continued)*

Activities	Inputs
1.1 Conduct an inventory of all SWEs (individual and organized) 1.2 Support the formation of two water user associations and two SWE cooperatives or associations 1.3 Establish links between groups and NWSC to support licensing as providers of water in the area either as franchise or sub-contracts or any other arrangement	Project staff NWSC Technical staff
2.1 Analyse SWEs' business performances and develop training manuals for SWEs 2.2 Conduct capacity-building courses on entrepreneurship for SWEs on business planning, customer service, and sanitary water handling 2.3 Capacity building on cooperative dynamics and governance and monitor gains achieved through improved business management 2.4 Link SWEs with business service providers for SWEs' entrepreneurship, growth and development, like formal credit	Consultant Project staff
3.1 Analysis of water sources, collection, delivery and payment, (supply chain) 3.2 Conduct a comprehensive water supply infrastructure survey on piping, supply points, selling points, and community water points within Maili Saba 3.3 Support tariff /consumer price control through negotiated prices 3.4 Enhance quality of water through appropriate handling 3.5 Support installation of water storage facilities to enhance reliability of water supply and handling	Technical water persons/artisans Project staff Consultants NWSC Nairobi City Council
4.1 Identify community initiatives towards poverty alleviation and water management and re-use 4.2 Develop a community water management tool for monitoring water use 4.3 Conduct participatory monitoring to assess improvement in service levels	Project staff NWSC Community
5.1 Organize stakeholders' consultative forums to deliberate on community water issues 5.2 Create linkages with other poor urban communities 5.3 Careful documentation of the project for possible replication, lessons learned and best practices 5.4 Continuous learning and process improvement on poor urban community water management	Community Project staff Consultants
Project monitoring Regular review Annual programme review End of programme review	Project staff Consultants

www.ingramcontent.com/pod-product-compliance
Lightning Source LLC
Chambersburg PA
CBHW080926050426
42334CB00055B/2800